SOMETHING FOR
THE WEEKEND, SIR?
(SFTWS)

SOMETHING FOR THE WEEKEND, SIR? (SFTWS)

*Lockdown, Leeds (Utd) and
Limiting Loneliness Through Laughter –
My Covid Journey – Stories and Joke Book
My 50th Year (and 51st) in Isolation*

STEVIE 'BOY' PARKER

The author of award-winning titles of
absolutely nowt else!!!

Dedicated to all those in the NHS and in memory of all those who lost their lives in the pandemic. Also, in memory of my Great-great Uncle John, who was indeed great. We were both grateful, perhaps, that he passed away just before it started ... surely, an ingratiated blessing.

And, of course, in memory of Queen Elizabeth II, RIP. God Save the King.

Foreword

Background/History

This 'newsletter'/communication started out as an opportunity to 'reach out' to work colleagues at the beginning of the pandemic, to keep people in touch and spirits up. Not everyone does Facebook/WhatsApp (they can be so transitive and 'here and now'); therefore, the initial idea to do something by email, allowing friends and colleagues to peruse at their leisure, seemed ideal.

Every newsletter has now been bound together into this one tome, and all net profits from this release of this publication will go to charity (St. Gemma's Hospice, Leeds). Please also see the final (and first listed) issue about 'Charity Walk' …

My 50th Year (and now a lot more) on the Planet!!! My Covid Journey

These last few years have been a bit strange for us all, given the pandemic. *Something for the Weekend, Sir* (SFTWS) started out as a short bulletin once a week ('for the weekend') as some humorous 'light relief' for colleagues. Later, it went bi-weekly and then to approximately once a month but longer … **much longer!!**

The COVID-19 Lockdown started on my 50th birthday in 2020, and SFTWS started that week. Covid restrictions ended almost two years later. This book was intended to be the end of SFTWS, pulling all issues together and encapsulating the Pandemic 'journey' through stories and laughter. But, of course, Covid didn't go quietly. Has it gone yet?!

The early versions were shorter and have developed over time but along the same theme of 'corny' jokes, quizzes, stories and anything in the news at the time. However, 40 issues later, it is still going strong and is now issued to hundreds of people.

As the pandemic persisted, I continued with the newsletter in a similar form. However, now that we seem to have put all Covid restrictions firmly behind us, it is time for me to bring it to a close … or is it?

Some explanations of **Key Features** are highlighted here. Mostly, however, are explained throughout the manuscript as we 'moved' through the weeks, months and YEARS!!!!

CCC – Comic Cone Chortle (originally titled as the attachment was in the shape of a cone) - This was attached to each edition of the original newsletter for use when you see the 🍦 sign. You could click the symbol to hear my voice… i.e. my Chuckle, Chortle or Hideous laugh!! This was supposed to be me laughing at my own jokes as some 'mates' say I like to do. Only available in the online version and was added retrospectively for the first few issues as did not officially appear until Issue 6.

(ᴗ|ᴗ) (ᴗ|ᴗ) (ᴗ|ᴗ) – These symbols are used throughout to indicate that there is a footnote. It is supposed to be a bum/bottom, meaning the bottom of the page. This is as crude as it gets!!!!!

AP – Audience Participation - A chance throughout to get some engagement with the audience. I was aiming for lots of genuine participation without 'forcing' anything.

Latest Edition First – I have deliberately started with the most recent edition(s) first. Highlighting the contrast (or not?) between then and now but also the similarities and us all going 'round in circles, etc.

Mrs Lena Backwell – A made-up pseudonym who writes about her fictitious husband. A sarcastic, acerbic and tongue-in-cheek view on the lockdown and 'Working from Homers'!!!!

The name apparently/allegedly was once (many years ago) a police equivalent of a 'John Doe' for 'Ladies of the night' when they were not forthcoming with their name!!!

Sammii – **Daughter**. 'Draws' for the Caption Competition and other elements. She has now graduated with Honours in Digital Art, as you will see in Issue No. 34. It genuinely takes me x10 longer to get her to do anything than for her to 'draw' it!!

Readers Reviews

"Looking at the scroll bar of this issue, I thought there must be pictures or something at the end, but, no, just crap jokes going on and on and on." - Col Capone

"As the world went mad and lockdown started, at least I had a week to see if I'd got the covid jokes this book is riddled with." - Poc

"A book that does the new stuff, the old stuff, and the funny stuff - well worth a chortle." - Mister Gin

"I received and read this every week - my sympathies are with the victims of Covid and the editor." - Ann Onomous

I'm not saying it's a painful read, but at last, something for the sadomasochists out there." - KA

"This is an exceptional record of how ordinary people lived through extraordinary times." - Sweeney Todd

"I shook my head so often at all the jokes, I had whiplash." - Mr P

SFTWS started during lockdown on my 50th birthday as a bit of fun and lasted for over two years!

Contents

Issue No 40

Wed 31st August 2022

Charity (Brother) Andy's Commemorative Walk Edition

We DID it!!!! FINAL ISSUE EVER

Leeds Utd Update – Brentford 5- 2 Leeds Ohhh dear!!!

Hi all,

CCC is attached for the final time ever!!!! 😄

As I bring SFTWS to a close (or do I?), please don't forget that the original reason for the communication WAS to keep in touch. So, please do so if you need to.

A final update before going to 'print' …

The Charity 'Walk' is highlighted in this issue in the main BUT first an update on other aspects since the last edition –

- ► War in Ukraine continues to rage
- ► Cost of living continues to rise
- ► Covid infections start to fall. BUT is it over?
- ► PM Leadership Elections – beyond a joke!
- ► Leeds Utd stay up by the skin of their teeth, and I've already had another comment of 'Are We Safe Yet?' – see Issue No. 31!!!

Before the 'walk,' let me first attempt to sum up all of the above in a nutshell.

Chaos On Many Fronts

Despite the cost of living, it does remain popular 😆 and how can funeral companies blame any increases on the cost of living? 😆 Indeed, a grave situation.

Apparently, Norway currently has the highest cost of living in Europe. There's Norway I could A-Fjord to live there. 😆

Yes, the catastrophic war continues to rage in Ukraine with no end in sight. Inflation, cost of living and energy prices continue to soar. A major crisis is around the corner if it's not already in the street and at the front door OR squeezing itself through the letter box!!! The imminent energy rises are NO laughing matter and the only thing that comes to mind (mentioned in an earlier issue, I'm sure) is the message I once saw when I was about five on a souvenir in a Blackpool gift shop … Save Gas, Fart in a Moneybox. 😆

To be fair, as the Tories fight over who should be PM, they have not come up with any better alternative to date. As we go to 'print,' we have yet another PM - the 3rd in three months!!! And the calls to continue/bring back SFTWS are deafening!!!

The Charity Three Peaks Walk – Sunday 14th August 2022

Firstly, thanks to all those sponsoring me/us. There is

still time for those who wish to do so.

Short story, we did it!!! We had three big problems, but after nearly 25 miles and 10+ hours we got over them. 😄

Slightly longer story. Let me summit up!!

The decision to stay the night before backfired as nobody got much sleep. This was due to a combination of warm conditions, strange surroundings, snoring, farting (mostly mine!!!) and midges keeping us awake.

Set Off and First Peak, Whernside – Long and Arduous!!

Anyway, after a bacon butty and a sausage roll, we managed to set off on time at 7 am up the highest peak, Whernside. Not wanting to peak too early, we started steadily and together as a group.

The sun shone unrelenting all day, but we didn't throw in the towel, other than into the cold bucket of water at every available stop. I lost almost ½ a stone over the course of the day but have put more back on as I don't think I've stopped eating or drinking since. 😄

Jelly babies would become the order and sweet of the day to keep our sugar levels up. One mate and fellow walker, would you believe, had more giant-size family bags than he did water which weighed nearly 3kg alone. His intention, of course, was to share, but still, it was a bit weighty and excessive in my opinion. Even before this, his bag (an old-fashioned sports bag) was heavier when empty than mine was full!!! A mouthful of jelly babies would also help with the sweet-talking needed to get us through later in the day. 😄

I set off behind my mate Nicholas at the start before overtaking him and leaving the see-Nick route behind. (Perhaps this should be the 'see-Nick's behind' route.) 😄 Whernside was tricky going up but much harder coming down until we started to get into a rhythm and the 'zone.'

At 10 am, the first 'Pit' stop came into view and the 'mirage' of our mobile support tuck shop, manned by our mate and Godsend Rob. He fussed over us for a few mins when all we really wanted was to be left alone. He'd kindly made us a concoction of energy drinks in a bowl with loads of ice that helped immensely. Stood waiting in the queue, I suppose this was the punchline. 😄 Shame there were no vodka or spirits in it!!!

Second Peak, Ingleborough – Sheer Muscle Burner!!

As we all started to spread out as a group, we nearly got lost a couple of times on the second peak. I did get the map thrown at me at one point but at least I knew where I stood. 😄

Then Ingleborough was next, which was sheer, steep and a real muscle burner going up and long and tedious coming down. By the end of the second stage, we had split up quite a lot, so some needed to wait while others caught up at Horton and our final stop. Resting, however, wasn't always good, as getting going again was tough. There was a perfect L-shaped corner out of the sun under a tree. Wow, 90 degrees in the shade. 😑

Pen-y-Ghent – Steep and Stays Steep!!

But get going again we did and onto the last Peak, Pen-y-Ghent. It started off steep from the start, continued steep and went on steep all the way to the top. Obviously, there is no easy way to do them all in a day, but this does seem a tough one to do last. Perhaps that was just the accumulative build-up.

After the top, it was all downhill from there and very hard on the feet, but we had been walking for nearly 10 hours by then. The sun continued to bake, and it seemed hotter near the end than it did at noon. At least high up, there was a little breeze that gave some relief, but once you were at sea level, it was tricky to catch your breath.

The last 1.5 miles (which felt like 10) were a nightmare. It was flat terrain, but every step was tough as you couldn't seem to find a decent place to put your next stride. Unfortunately, 5 pm was also the hottest part of the day (or seemed to be).

The terrain and the trek weren't funny; they were hill areas 😑. But we made it through with sore feet, lost plenty of weight (best diet ever) and achy bodies (that kicked in especially two days afterwards).

We made it back, peeled shoes and socks off, had a shower and then went for a beer!!! Obviously, there are no photos of me in the shower as I have selfie steam problems. 😆 Some struggled to eat much at dinner, BUT I managed my usual feast. However, after all that alphabet soup and spaghetti, I did have a large vowel movement the next day. 😂

To (sort of) quote Sir Steven Redgrave. Never again … until we do it next time!!!!!

At the time of going to press, we have raised over £3k and counting for St. Gemma's Hospice. We will be doing a photoshoot this weekend with a 'big cheque.' Now see below.

Byeeeeeeeeeeeee

Steve (Parker)

Issue No 39

Wed 3rd May 2022

Daughter's 27th Birthday &
2nd Anniversary Edition

Nearly the End

Headlines:

▶   And now the end is (very) near!!

Leeds Utd Update – Leeds 0-4 Manchester City

And now the end is near

And now, the end is near
And so I write the final chapter
My readers, I'll say it clear
I've always stated my case of which you're after
I've lived a life that's full
I travelled and worked for England's Highways
But more, much more than this
I said it my way

Stories and gags, there's been a few (thousand)
But then again, too few to mention
I said what I had to say

And saw it through without invention (just
plagiarism)
I (sort of) planned each chapter and verse
Each careful step through the dreaded Covid
But more, much more than this
I said it my way

Yes, there were times, I'm sure you knew
When I went on more than I should do
But through it all, when there was doubt
I wrote it up and sent it out
I faked it all, and yet I stood tall
And did it my way

I've made you love, laugh and cry
You've now had your fill
And now, as tears subside
you must think what you can do for others
Just think, I did all this
And may I say, not in a shy way
Oh no, no, not for me
I did it for chaaaaarity!!!!!

For what is a man, what has he got
If not himself then he has not
To say all the things he truly feels
And not the words of one who kneels

The record shows, I took the blows
But NOW it's your way (turn).

Then, and only THEN, are you allowed to say 'Stop'!!!!
SEE Issue No 1, March 2020.

In other words, say Yes to charity and END SFTW and
S!!!!

THE END OF THE END!!!!!!!!!!!!!!!??????????

Yes, hopefully, this is the end of the pandemic (for now) and, therefore, the end of the SFTWS/Newsletter.

Every newsletter has now been bound together into one tome, and all net profits will go to charity (St. Gemma's Hospice, Leeds).

Hopefully, this book will be published soon after my late brother's Charity Walk in September 2022, who, as many know (and as highlighted in various editions), passed away in 2010. The walk was supposed to take place as a 10-year commemorative anniversary edition, but of course, because of Covid, it has been delayed by two years. Keep your eyes 'peeled' for this event.

Cheers.

All t' Best!

Take care.

Byeeeeeeeeeeeeeeeeeeeeee!!!!

Stevie

Issue No 38

Wed 23rd March 2022

Two Years on and
My Birthday
(Again!!!!!!)

Headlines:

- ► War in Ukraine continues to Rage
- ► Stevie Gets Covid
- ► Two Years on and Restrictions Finally Lifted

Leeds Utd Update
Wolves 2-3 Leeds, Leeds 2-1
Norwich … WOW!!!!!

Hi all … CCC attached for your pleasure when you see this sign. 😆

It's nearly time for a get together, surely??!!!!!!!!! 👣

Well, would you Adam and Eve it? The unthinkable has happened. No, not the outbreak of war in Europe or Bielsa being sacked… BUT…

After nearly two years, I have Covid!!!!!!!!!

As you know, Covid/SFTWS started two years ago (on my birthday), and now I have tested positive just before another birthday. What a birthday pressie. Does this mean another birthday celebration I have to cancel?? It's just not fair!!!

Thanks for asking!!! I'm fine, though. As you know, I am quite a positive person. BUT now my positivity is helping, given I'm now positive that I'm positive!!! (‿|‿) X1

In Other News –

▶ Yes, Leeds sack Bielsa after three glorious years and then we finally win a game (just!!!!) after six straight defeats. Then Leeds win again in an amazing comeback against Wolves. Hopefully, won't need to rely on Chelski being deducted 50 points for dodgy Russian owners for Leeds to stay up. 😆

▶ War continues to rage in Ukraine, but even before the first missile was fired, Macron rushed to Moscow to unconditionally surrender. 😆

▶ Ferry Company arbitrarily sacks 800 staff - see Under the RADAR. In protest, I'm not practising the 'piano' (see below) for a while!!!!!!

In this Issue –

▶ Petrol Prices Rocket (Fuels Inflation) – 'Car Owner Virus'

▶ P& P& P&O, P&O, P&O - I am the Music/ Redundancy Man - Ferry Redundancies. NOT Ferry Funny

▶ Ukraine War/Invasion

▶ Bielsa – The Living Legend

- ▶ What We've Missed Since the Last Issue –
  - » Prince Andrew – Closure for Now
  - » V-Day
- ▶ Stevie's Puuuuuzzles of the Week!!
- ▶ Under the RADAR (Random Alert Detailing Alternative Reports)
- ▶ Next Issue (There isn't one) and Next Week's TV
- ▶ (‿|‿)(‿|‿)(‿|‿)

Petrol Prices Rocket (Fuels Inflation) – 'Car Owner Virus'

It's not just tyres that are suffering from inflation at garages as the price of petrol continues to escalate. Customers are sweating at the pumps and anxious about the price they need to pay. Is this the first sign of … Car Owner Virus? 😂 Every time I go to the garage, I do get rather emotional, though. I just start filling up. 😂

Q. Do we fill up the tank or buy Chelski football club? See below. At current prices, don't fill up on petrol unless you must – it's a very fuelish thing to do!!! One good thing about the price is it does, perhaps, stop Kurt Zouma from pouring it on his cat and setting it on fire. The only way you can get a cat to go woof. 😂

See also Under the RADAR … 'Zoumar is charged.'

Finally, there is apparently a new crime wave sweeping the nation. Robbing petrol stations. Not for the cash, just taking the petrol and doing a runner.

Q – Do you still hear the sea if you hold up a Shell? 😂

And don't forget, Baby Spice can't steal much petrol, but Geri can. 😂

P& P& P&O, P&O, P&O 😂 - I Am The Music/Redundancy Man – Ferry Redundancies

🎵 I am the Redundancy man, and I come from down your waterway. What can I play? I play the underhand P&O Redundancy Card. 🎵😂

Not many are singing this tune, and it's certainly no ferry-tale for P&O workers who are laid off to make way for 'economical realignment.' Another phrase, of course, for just sacking them to bring in cheaper workers.

Q - What is brown and comes out of cows backwards?

The Isle of Wight Ferry. 😂 NOT ferry funny, I know! Oops. I've done that one!!

Chelski on the Slippery Slopes???

As well as a couple of wins for Leeds, some further good news for Leeds' fans is the troubles for Chelsea atm. Unbelievable, but Chelski suggested that the recent FA Cup Match at Middlesbrough should be played behind closed doors as they couldn't sell any tickets to fans due to the restrictions. They said it would be 'Sporting Integrity' to do so, as they put it. Unbelievable, Jeff!!! Most Chelsea fans have just decided to support Newcastle now. 😂

In the end, they all travelled up for the FA Cup match for a quid each (not the Harry Potter game) on the Megabus. 😄

Ukraine War/Invasion

Many supermarkets have renamed Chicken Kiev to Kyiv in support of the Ukrainians. And who says the (John) West aren't doing enough? 😄

Who would have thought that after two years of Covid, as one threat starts to decline, another one starts big time!!!! We are now experiencing the invasion of an independent, European sovereign state by Russia and putting the world on a knife edge.

Embargos, bans and sanctions are now being enforced on Russia, but there is no sign of a ceasefire. Even the streaming services are pulling out of Russia. The only one they have now is Nyetflix. 😄

Lots of Russian comedians are making jokes about Putin; they aren't that good, but the execution will be worse!! One of them is saying if Russia takes away Ukraine's nuclear bombs, they'll just end up with depleted Ukranium. 😄

Bielsa – The Living Legend

What a legend, on and off the pitch. There really is not anyone else like him. Who else could turn Leeds into everyone else's second fave team? It was genuinely reported that he was considering playing a new formation if he'd stayed for another year. Would you believe the new formation was three at the back but the middle defender being the goalkeeper (sic).

What We've Missed Since the Last Issue –

> » Prince Andrew. To finally close this down (for now)

He settles out of court. In summary …

🎵 Ohhhhhhh, the grand old Duke of York, he borrowed 12 million quid. He gave it to someone he'd never ever met, and for something he never did. 🎵 😂

> » Valentine's Day

Valentine's Day has been and gone. I made a bird table for the missus, but only putting her in 5th place didn't please her. 😂

> » RIP Shane Warne

Shane Warne, the leading wicket-taker of all time, has made his final delivery, pulled up stumps and passed away in his early 50s. This was just hours after leading the tributes to another Australian cricketer Rodney Marsh who died the day before.

Under the RADAR (Random Alert Detailing Alternative Reports)

BOJO is still putting his feet in it!!!

https://www.theguardian.com/politics/2022/mar/21/drawing-parallels-between-brexit-and-war-in-ukraine

Zouma is charged!!

https://www.thesun.co.uk/sport/17968690/kurt-zouma-charged-rspca-cat-kick-video/

USA Trump China by flying the flag!!

https://www.theguardian.com/us-news/2022/mar/07/donald-trump-russia-ukraine-jets-chinese

Speaking of flags, I've done a DIY course in semaphore this week. After 8 hours, I'm really starting to flag. 😑

🎵 Stevie's Puuuuuzzles (and Last Week's Answers) of the Week 🎵 👬

▶ What have the start dates of the First World War, Second World War and the Russian Invasion got in common? Clue. Is it coincidence or catastrophe? **See (‿|‿) X3**

Next Issue and Next Week's TV

▶ Next Issue – There isn't one!!!!!!

TV

▶ Cat Ballou – Great Classics, Wed 30th 11.15 pm
▶ Withnail & I – Film 4, Fri 1st April 1.45 am

All t' best. Take care

Cheers.

THE END!!!!!!! (‿|‿) X2

Steve

(⌣|⌣) **X1** I have been Covid negative for a few days by the time you read this.

(⌣|⌣) **X2** Or as Winnie (Not Mandela – close, but no cigar 😄) once said … 'Is it the end, the beginning of the end or just the end of the beginning?'

(⌣|⌣) **X3** World War I started on 28 July 1914 after tensions in Europe came following the assassination of Archduke Franz Ferdinand.

When you add up the numbers of the date – 28+7+19+14 – you get 68.

World War II, which became the deadliest conflict in human history, started on 1 September 1939.

And when you add up the date – 1+9+19+39 – you're once again left with 68.

The same goes for the start of Russia's attack on Ukraine, which kicked off on 24 February 2022 – 24+2+20+22 = 68.

Issue No 37
Mon 31st Jan 2022

Headlines:
- ► Ukraine Under Threat
- ► BJ Still Not in the Clear!!!

Leeds Utd Update
Leeds 0-1 Newcastle,
Sat 22nd Jan

Hi all … CCC is attached for your pleasure when you see this sign. 😄

How are you? Not rhetorical!!! 👥👥

Footy and Leeds

As always, I'll kick off with footy, and it must be time for SFTWS, given that Leeds have won a couple of games. Unfortunately, we couldn't make it a hat-trick of wins with a dismal result against Newcastle. A win would have gone a long way to securing 'safety.' At least Leeds managed to sign someone in the transfer 'window' - the North Korean International … Fook In No Wan. 😄

Blue Tory Rage Continues over Boris. The 'Eyes' have it; the 'Eyes' have it!!!!!!!!!!!!!!!!!!!!!!

50 Shades of Gray and Savid's Sibling

Perhaps, Sue Gray's final Party Gate Report can tell us if Leeds will stay up.

Everyone is saying it will answer everything else!!!

Apparently, Savid Javid's brother is heading up the Met investigation (sic). Unbelievable!!!! https://www.mirror.co.uk/news/politics/met-police-stitch-up-claim-26102172.

Supposedly, BJ used the 'Shade of Gray' paint when refurbishing his flat. It'll cover up everything. 😂

Breaking News – Making Whoopi!!!

Finally, at going to press, Whoopi Goldberg in holocaust comment controversy. Like the woman in the orthopaedic shoe, she 'stands corrected.' 😂

https://people.com/tv/whoopi-goldberg-apologizes-on-the-view-after-holocaust-comment-controversy-i-stand-corrected/

In this Issue –

- ▶ BJ the 'Party' Leader's 'UK Reign' Under Threat as 'Ukraine' is Under Threat by Russia
- ▶ Pressure Mounts on BJ –
    - » Gray Report is not Black and White – Just the Former (as Most is Redacted)
    - » Would I Lie to You – Is He the Party Leader?!
    - » Who Let the Dogs Out – Afghan Hounds or People?
- ▶ No More Birthdays or Cakes for Barry Cryer – RIP
- ▶ NATO and Russia – Playing Chicken in Kiev
    - » 'Put In' Perspective
- ▶ Barry Cryer – RIP
    - » The 'Ultimate Parrot' Joke
- ▶ His Royal Lowness Formerly known as Prince, Loses Titles
    - » Court Case Looms – 'And Ruse' Past Actions/ Acquaintances
- ▶ Fraud … Minister Resigns
- ▶ Stevie's Puuuuuzzles of the Week!! Back Next Week
- ▶ Under the RADAR (Random Alert Detailing Alternative Reports)
- ▶ Next Edition and Next Week's TV
- ▶ (⌣|⌣)(⌣|⌣)(⌣|⌣)

BJ's UK Reign Under Threat as Ukraine is Under Threat as Russia and NATO Play Chicken in Kiev 😂

Shambolic shenanigans in Whitehall as the Govt continues to be paralysed with major distractions still unresolved. The Sue Gray Report is finally published (in part) as going to press with this issue. The boot is Putin by Nato in Ukraine.

Pressure Mounts on 'Party Leader' BJ

New boozy revelations revealed that the Cabinet dressed up as members of Group YMCA to attend and join another party … the 'Labour' Party. 😂

> » Gray Report is not Black and White – Just Black (as Most is Redacted) 😂

As normal, Govt is put on hold whilst everyone continues to await the Gray Report, even though there are many pressing issues. Faith in all politics and public sector services continues to nosedive.

> » Would I Lie to You – Is He the Party Leader?!

Taking his role as party leader a bit far, BJ continues to sink further in the Drowning Street mess as Sue Gray's Report is finally published (in part). Perhaps Operation 'Save Big Dog' conclusion by Tory MPs is that he needs to be put down. BYOB and a cake to the next party: Johnson's Leaving do. 😂

The PM was set to appear on 'Would I Lie to You,' but producers pulled the plug on the basis that the contestants wouldn't have a choice to make. 😂

♫ I suppose BJ will say, 'It's my (Conservative) Party, and I'll lie if I want to, lie if I want to, lie if I want to. You would have cake too, if you haven't a clue!! ♫

BJ is like the Eskimo who started a fire in his canoe ... he wants his kayak and heat it!!! And, of course, he ends up down the creek without a paddle. ☺

» Who Let the Dogs Out – Afghan Hounds or People?

Sticking with song quotes, or more precisely, who exactly did get the hounds out? There's more controversy as a senior official sheds light on the claim that BJ sanctioned the 'Pets Before People' evacuation of Afghanistan.

» No More Birthdays or Cakes for Barry Cryer - RIP

As you know, SFTWS/Lockdown started on my birthday (and Barry Cryer's, see below!!!!) in 2020. We now know that all restrictions will end on the 24th of March. I will, therefore, miss three celebrations (25, given that I celebrate every month!!!). So, I'm one of the many disgruntled. But many have missed sooooo much more.

NATO and Russia - Playing Chicken in Kiev

As tensions mount in Ukraine, another leader in difficulty is the Russian Premier. When repeatedly asked about Put in troops on the border near the water bank. All he could say was ... 'Crimea River.' ☺

» 'PUT IN' Perspective

To be fair, talks are continuing, but the Russian leader is under considerable pressure back home. There is a suggestion that this show of strength is just to deflect from his own faltering ratings and unpopularity. He was recently stopped on the Ukraine border by passport control and asked the usual questions.

'Name ...?'

"Vladimir Putin."

'Occupation ...?'

"No, just visiting." 😂

Barry Cryer - RIP

Barry C, one of the most prolific comedy writers and star of the comedy show 'I'm Sorry I Haven't a Clue' for 50 years, died last week. His appearance on this show was just an act, as opposed to the PM - which is more like a mission statement. 😂

I never realised that Bazza and I had so much in common. Barry was Born In 'Leeds, Leeds, Leeds' on 23rd March (yes, same place and day as Me, Me Me), wrote hilarious gags and was a comedy genius (well, two out of three isn't bad for similarities). These similarities were genuinely unknown to me until his sad, sudden death this week.

» The 'Ultimate' Parrot Joke

Cryer claimed his 'ultimate' parrot joke was published

in 2020 in The Oldie magazine.

The joke describes a woman who purchases a parrot for only £5.

"Well, I must confess, it was brought up in a brothel," says the shopkeeper. "And, to put it politely, it has quite an extensive vocabulary."

"Never mind," says the woman. "At that price, I'll take it."

So, she takes the parrot home, puts its cage in the living room and takes the cover off.

"New place – very nice," says the parrot.

Then the woman's two daughters walk in.

"New place, new girls – very nice," says the parrot.

Then the woman's husband walks in, and the parrot says, "Oh, hello, Bob!"

His Royal Lowness, Formerly Known as Prince, Loses Titles and More!!!

No crying rivers here as the man formerly known as Prince continues to be dethroned … no sweat!!!

Court Case Looms – 'And Ruse' Past Actions/ Acquaintances (⌣|⌣) X1

Another man in a bit of hot water and losing his titles faster than Lance Armstrong 🚴 (⌣|⌣) X2 but still not sweating, is His Royal Lowness. He's even lost his honorary title to St Andrews Golf Club (sic).

FRAUD – Minister Resigns in Unusual Sign of Decency and Responsibility

https://www.theguardian.com/politics/2022/jan/24/minister-resigns-in-protest-at-handling-of-fraudulent-covid-loans

Moving from frauds to fraud, is another story completely overshadowed by Partygate. Minister Lord Agnew resigned after billions of pounds were given to bogus companies and are now to be written off. Shadowy schemes are being wholly overshadowed by everything else going on. All this time, allowing firms to claim when they didn't even exist!!! Apparently, a lot of this money was reinvested in Egypt ... it must have been a pyramid scheme. 😂

As a counter-fraud civil servant in customs, I once had to check Czech cheques at Check-in. One day a man came up to me and 'went' ... bawk, bawk, bawk, bawk. 'Surely, Steve, you aren't doing the 'Sorry, sir, this is the Check-in Desk' joke again, are you?' Nope, apparently not. 😂

But seriously, did you hear about the midget fortune teller who is on the run after making millions from misleading people on the outcome of the above case? 'Surely, Steve, you aren't trying to do the 'small medium at large' joke headline again, are you?' Nope, apparently not. 😂 Apparently, she's now started pinching t-shirts in the order of size ... small medium still at large. 😂

🎵 Stevie's Puuuuuzzles 🎵 👥

Back properly next week. Just a quick one for this week ...

► If there is a conflict in Ukraine and a plane crashes on the border of Ukraine and Russia. In which country will they bury the survivors?

Please see the Answers section at the back of the book for this week's puzzle.

Under the RADAR (Random Alert Detailing Alternative Reports).

Driving Miss Daily!!!! Man drives without a licence every day for 70 years (sic).

https://www.bbc.co.uk/news/uk-england-nottinghamshire-60159649

Bloody Sunday. 50 Years on Remembered

https://www.bbc.co.uk/news/uk-northern-ireland-60130409

Sunday Bloody Sunday. Classic Alan Partridge https://www.youtube.com/watch?v=6RTJ4vH0YUs

Next Issue and Next Week's TV

TV

► Blake 7/Man from Atlantis/Surgical Spirits

You can catch many of these 'blasts from the past' on 'Forces TV.' Blake 7 is hardly classic TV, hasn't aged well and can be rather embarrassing with acting, plot and 'special effects.' BUT, I'm hooked again on a show from my youth.

Does anyone else remember it and/or are watching it again? 👀

Next Week

- ▶ More on 'Partygate,' I'm sure. Will BJ survive???!!!!
- ▶ Changes to the Highway Code. No need for pedestrians/cyclists to look both ways anymore. If they get hit, it's the driver's fault, whatever the circumstances!!

All t' best.

Steve

(⌣|⌣) **X1** – almost used … (Finger) Prints And Ruse Past Actions/Acquaintances. Perhaps, a little too contrived!!!! **What do ya think?????**

(⌣|⌣) **X2** - **Lance Edward Armstrong** (né **Gunderson**; born September 18, 1971) is an American former professional road racing cyclist. Armstrong was stripped of his seven consecutive Tour de France titles from 1999 to 2005 after a doping investigation and his admission to using performance-enhancing drugs.

Issue No 36

Wed 8th Dec 2021

Headlines:

- ▶ PM Accused of Lying, Aides Laugh at Xmas Parties
- ▶ Afghan Dog Rescue – Cover Up

Leeds Utd Update
Leeds 2-2 Brentford,
Sun 5th Dec

Hi all ... CCC is attached for your pleasure when you see this sign. 😄

Stevie is back!!!!! Apologies for my absence for soooooo long; I'll not let it happen again. I've been waiting until Leeds finally won a game, again!!! Two late goals helped us to four points, but we are still in the mire.

A quick one to get back into the swing, and I think there needs to be another along soon on a few subjects that are looming/erupting!!!! There might be plenty to go at.

This next photo amused me. For no reason, really, other than I think it sums up our times. 😄

Covid Omicron New Measures – Here We Go Again!!! And the Smell of Bacon and Poop

Further measures are brought in even though cases don't seem to be that high - yet!!!! But was there another reason?! More acquaintances seem to have (or have had) Covid than ever before. Apparently, the worst/weirdest symptom is the loss of taste and/ or smell. As we know, we don't know what we have 'til it's gone. The inability to smell a bacon butty or perhaps even a poopy nappy (or BO) is more of an inconvenience than you can imagine, apparently. Can't you just reset to olfactory settings? And the inability to taste one's own food is even worse. This would be my nightmare.

Footy

I'll kick off, as usual, with football. Leeds win then draw but are still in danger, with some tough fixtures coming up. As Halloween comes and goes, however, the real horror show is at Old Trafford as Man U are battered by Liverpool and then Man City. But the hammering against Watford finally puts the nail in Solskjaer's coffin. Their new manager's reign started with the weirdest goal from Arsenal that you will ever see – see Under the RADAR. Even though their form has now improved, I'm still not missing the chance to get a dig in at their recent woes. It takes my mind off Leeds' woes, I suppose.

There's been a slight gap since the last one for a 'little breather' (**see (‿|‿) X1**) as we move from 'dealing' with Covid to 'living' with it. Perhaps, we can start to wear our shoes out quicker than slippers again soon. This should mean that I can also start to transition and organise events and promote local offers.

So, What's Been Going On Since the Last Issue?

- ▶ Sir Kev – 101 miles in 24 Hours
- ▶ Man U in Turmoil
- ▶ Shortages
  - » Petrol – Is the Crisis Over? Your Gas is as Good as Mine (‿|‿) X2)
  - » Lorry Drivers and Their Lorries
  - » Abattoir – What an Offal Crisis – Pigs not

Facing the/a Chop

» Energy Prices – Soaring

▶ Shatner in Space – To Oldly Go Where No Man and all that!!!
(◡|◡) x3)

▶ Stevie's Puuuuuzzles of the Week!! Star Trek Jokes.

▶ Under the RADAR (Random Alert Detailing Alternative Reports)

▶ Next Edition and Next Week's TV

▶ (◡|◡)(◡|◡)(◡|◡)

Sir Kev – 101 Miles in 24 hours!!!!!!!!!!!!!!!!!!!!!!!!!

The word 'legend' is often overused, but I don't think so in the case of (Sir) Kev (Sinfield). He has now raised over £2m for charity – see/donate in Under the RADAR below. It's only a matter of time before his title becomes permanent, surely. What a legend!!! I once came out of a pub late at night, and a very drunk woman said to me 'Stevie P... you are an effing ledge.' I still have no idea how long mi mam had been there or who she was with. 😄 **(See (◡|◡) X4)**

Man U in Turmoil

With another manager in place, what are the similarities between Man U, Black Eyed Peas and Prince Andrew? They have all been rubbish since Fergie left. 😄

Man U's Maguire was sent off recently and was set to miss the Chelsea game – BUT Chelsea appealed the decision. 😄

After the first debacle against Liverpool, they tried to get some composure back with an updated game of What Time Is it Mr Wolf? ('It's five past De Gea' 😄) and watching a remake of an old classic when Harry (Maguire) met Salah. 😄

Shortages
» Petrol – Is the Crisis Over? Your Gas Is as Good as Mine. 😄

BBC Reporter Phil McCann (sic) reports on the petrol crisis (see below), and most of the Spice Girls can't fill up (so run out) … but Geri can. 😄

I decided not to pay that petrol price on that day, so I just pumped up my car tyres instead … and the guy charged me a quid. I said, "It was only 20p last week." He said, "That's the price of inflation." 😄

https://www.joe.ie/news/bbc-reporter-phil-mccann-responds-going-viral-731967

Shortages seem to be over for the moment, but the price is continuing to rise.
» Lorry drivers and Their Lorries

There didn't seem to be much of a shortage at the tongue Twisters annual gathering as many were mentioning seeing a red lorry followed by a yellow lorry followed by a red lorry. 😄

One of them was just about to run over a couple of

STDs when one said to the other ... I'm a gonna ere. 😅

It genuinely does seem to be less of an issue atm, but everyone still has delays to delivery, and surely this can only get worse in the run-up to Crimbo.

> » Abattoirs – What an Offal Crisis – Pigs Don't Face the Chop

As the slaughterhouse crisis deepens, is it a misteak NOT to allow visas, or is the Govt just raising the steaks on a job not well done? 😅

> » Energy Bills Soaring as More Firms Run out of Steam

As the lights are turned off on more and more energy firms – another crisis looms. People are asked to fart in a money box to save gas 😅 (appropriately (‿|‿) X5), and fish and chips are the order of the day as we all look for anything battery. 😅

Shatner in Space – To Oldly Go Where No Man Has Gone Before!!!

♫ **Stevie's Puuuuuzzles of the Week!!** ♫

Star Trek 'Jokes'

To boldly laugh like we've never laughed before. I'm sure you can work most of them out.

- ► How does a Romulan frog stay camouflaged?
- ► What did Mr Spock find in Captain Kirk's toilet?

- How many ears does Captain Kirk have?
- What is Commander Riker's favourite hobby?
- Where do the Borg go to eat fast food?
- What's it called when a crew member on Deep Space 9 runs as fast as he can?
- What are glasses called on planet Vulcan?
- How do you stop yourself from falling out of a Bird of Prey?
- What do you call two science officers having an argument?
- If Spock has pointy ears, then what does Scotty have?
- Why is Star Trek so successful?
- What illness did everyone on the Enterprise catch that made them red and itchy?
- Why did Riker die from friendly fire?
- What did Scotty say when little shards of ice began hitting the Enterprise?
- Why was Captain Picard so confused when the android disappeared?

Please see the Answers section at the back of the book for the punchlines.

I'll leave you with: "A split infinitive walks into a bar … to boldly go where no infinitive has gone before." 😂

Under the RADAR (Random Alert Detailing Alternative Reports)

PC takes the biscuit!!!!

https://www.bbc.co.uk/news/uk-england-leeds-58904606

Customers have to make their beds!!!

https://www.euronews.com/2021/12/02/ikea-store-in-denmark-hosts-snow-stranded-customers-overnight

You can donate online 24 hours a day at https://donate.giveasyoulive.com/fundraising/kevin-sinfields-the-extra-mile-challenge. You can also donate £3 by texting the word (Sir) Kevin to 70143.

https://www.givemesport.com/1796431-smith-rowe-goal-vs-man-utd-the-13-craziest-goals-in-premier-league-history.

Next Issue and Next Week's TV

TV

Unforgiven – Thursday 9th December 10.30 pm C5

The Manchurian candidate, BBC4 9 pm

Xmas Issue, More Lockdown and To Party or Not to Party!!!!!

Take Care.

Stevie

(‿|‿) **X1**

(‿|‿) **X2)** Worth another 'Airing'!!!

(‿|‿) **X3)** Pinched by Private Eye (again)!!!

(‿|‿) **X4)** Spookily, I share my birthday with five Sirs of Sport. Sir Roger Bannister, Sir Chris Hoy, Sir Jason Kenny, Sir Steven Redgrave and Sir Mo Farah. Mine (like Sir Kev's) is only a matter of time?!

(‿|‿) **X5)** I always remember this in a shop window – on a trip to Blackpool when I was about 6. Over 30 years ago now!!!!

Issue No 35

Late, Late August Football and Afghan Transfer Deadline Edition

Leeds' Latest Deadline Day Signing?!

Headlines:
- ▶ Taliban take control of Kabul/Airport
- ▶ Storms batter America

Leeds Utd Update - Leeds 1-1
Burnley, 29th Aug

Hi all ... CCC is attached for your pleasure when you see this sign. 😂

I should have got it out earlier (oo-err) but paid the price given that 'Private Eye' have now nicked one of my jokes (see 'no TV for Afghans' below). You DO know my view on plagiarism, though???!!!!!

Feedback (from last issue) –

No 1 –
- ► Firstly, results from the poll - Should I continue?
    - » 2 - Yes
    - » 1 - Don't know
    - » 4 - 'Spoilt' papers – they have been given everything they had ever wanted since they were a 'scrap' of paper(boy). 😂

   Said comments couldn't be reproduced here!!!

    - » 56667 - Abstained/no reply

Once again, a clear majority!!!!

No 2 –
- ► 'Morning Steve, and thanks again for sending these out.

I know I don't normally reply, but that "show my bare bum in Woolworths window/Town Hall Steps" from the last issue reminded me of the story about Bernie Slaven in Middlesbrough. It's not Woolies, but it's as close as you can get:

48

https://www.gazettelive.co.uk/news/local-news/bernie-bares-soul-more-3796944

Steve Bish.'

In this Issue –

▶ Opening-Up with Opening-Up: From Confusion to Bliss

▶ Afghans Hounded in Transfer Day Deadline
  » The US Withdrawal - Biden HIS Time?!
  » No TV for Afghans - New Regime Enforced by Teleban 🙄
  » Not a Cock and (Ka)Bul Story

▶ Storms – Ida Downs the US and Covers East Coast
  » Bazza Manilow Off Mid-Song in Mime Blowing Incident – 'We Made it Through the Rain' (NOT!!)

▶ Caption Comp – Results

▶ NEW FEATURE (as promised) – THE Coin of Cidence

▶ 🎵 Stevie's Puuuuuzzles of the Week!! 🎵

▶ Under the RADAR (Random Alert Detailing Alternative Reports).

▶ Next Edition and Next Week's TV

▶ (⌣|⌣)(⌣|⌣)(⌣|⌣)

Opening Up with Opening Up: From Confusion to Bliss

Cases and deaths are up again, and thousands of positive test results were found discarded at BH Music Festivals (see Under the RADAR).

Confusion is summed up by my two mates (??). They are the extremes of the spectrum when it comes to Covid 'Caution' –

► One is in that river in Egypt, even though his best mate has just had it – and he's in denial that he's 'had it' as well😂.The other is completely paranoid, quarantines his post for a week and has just bought another fridge (sic), so he doesn't need to use the food that has just come in for a few days. All very bizarre!!!

Weirder still, he bought his second fridge and gave it to his wife for her recent birthday. He said, 'It's a strange present, I know, but you should have seen her face light up when she opened it'. 😂

Coincidentally, I might need a new fridge as well. When I came in late last night after a few beers, there was a note on mine from the missus that said … 'Sorry, this isn't working'. 😂

Wedding Bells. Even the Cake's in Tiers (Sorry, couldn't resist).

Speaking of mates, another one is having his wedding reception in Sept '21. This is more than a year after he got married. Another strange Covid situation.

He's gone from eating like a bachelor to eating as a husband. He now looks a lot 'healthier'!!! But, 'Benny Boy' is the first person in history to need a bigger suit between getting married and his wedding reception.

Afghans Hounded in Transfer Day Deadline

As Leeds Utd finally get their man (Dan James) on Transfer Day (2½ years late), chaos is the order of the day in Kabul as the US leave after 20 years.

» The US Withdrawal - Biden HIS Time?

The initial decision under Trump and confirmation under Biden to withdraw troops was obviously not thought through BUT the biggest mistake was the evacuation. Why was it not planned better and so chaotic? As one of my ex-colleagues always used to say (sic) as we got out of the lift too early after returning to the building after a fire drill … 'There's nothing worse than a premature evacuation.'

» No TV For Afghans

The new regime is apparently to be enforced by tellyban. Surely, they need something stricter than that. My joke has already been 'pinched' by Private Eye – See below and (‿|‿) X1).

"Bloody tellyban!"

> » Not a Cock and (Ka)bul Story – Bad Altitude
> in Cliff Hangar (OTT 😂?)

The scenes at the airport were even worse, but the idea of getting out of Kabul by hanging onto the outside of a plane … I don't think it will take off. 😂 Even with the aircraft in plane sight, thousands are left behind, and only those tripping over their luggage will go flying. 😂

Even a photon with no luggage at all couldn't get on a plane – and it was travelling light. 😂

Apologies, but I think my telling of airport jokes might be terminal. 😂

What Do We/They Want?

Anyway, as the crowds continue to shout……………

What do we want? Low flying airplane noises.
When do we want them?
NNNNNNNNEEEEEEEEEEEEEEOOOOOOOOOOWWWW. 😩

And even through all the chaos, Airport security are still making jokes about passports. You do have to hand it to them. 😩

Storms – Ida Downs USA and Covers East Coast

As Biden struggles with the basics of how many US Citizens there are and/or even his own name, what chance has he got with Afghanistan or the new flooding catastrophe?

The storms have left many Americans with only a part of their roof. Oof, that must be tough. 😩

My inbox has been flooded by storm jokes, but with 45 dead, it's no laughing matter – just like the criminalisation of Nitrous Oxide (see Under the RADAR). 😩 You might have to wait until the next issue, however, because all my storm jokes are just a draft atm. I think they'll blow you away, though. 😩

> » Bazza Manilow Off Mid-Song in Mime
>   Blowing Incident

It was during the previous storm, Henry, but still worth a mention. Bazza was interrupted halfway through his song/concert. Coincidentally, singing 'We Made it Through the Rain'... NOT 😩 (ᴗ|ᴗ) **X2.** https://www.express.co.uk/news/world/1480180/Hurricane-Henri-

Barry-Manilow-Homecoming-New-York-City-Central-Park-latest-news-vn

Dennis Pennis (DP)

Does anyone remember him?

Running after Bazza with a giant bedsheet asking if he'd dropped his hanky. 😆 My favourite, perhaps, was him asking Demi Moore, after the film Striptease had been released … 'If you were paid enough money and it was tastefully done, would you consider keeping your clothes on in a movie?' Cringeworthy, but Comedy Gold??!! **What was your fave?** **More DP next week, if you wish.**

Caption Competition - Results

As I said, there was an obvious one that a few managed to get (see Coin of Cidence below as well). It was, of course …

- Free Dom Day (or something on similar themes) as the last issue was the 'Freedom Day' Edition.

But the winner is Mags J, with –

BJ –It's always Meme, Meme, Meme with you … but, as you should know, it's all about Me, Me Me!!!! A net result for Boris!!!

A pint for Mags or a double vodka and slim.

Coin of Cidence – Does Your Flip Always 'Land' on Heads!?!

Some will say the only coincidence would be if there weren't any at all!!!?? Recent 'coins' worthy of a flip (I think) –

- See the Caption Comp above. This was drafted weeks before the previous issue and yet gave the perfect caption for Free Dom Day!!
- I was doing my 'Couch to 5k Challenge.' Halfway through, the bell rang to say 50% complete. At the same time, Bon Jovi sings (on Spotify) singing 'You are halfway there'!!!
- I went for a coffee, and the music in my headphones was the same Billy Joel song 'Light the Fire' as in the shop (plus, it was not on the radio).
- As I redraft this, the film Serendipity (not worth watching) is on …

'That's enough 'Coins' for this week, Steve'!!!!

Tell me yours and/or do you agree they happen or not? 👥

🎵 Stevie's Puuuuuzzles
(and Last Week's Answers)
of the Week 🎵 👥

This Week's Quiz -

Here are a couple of quick quizzes involving audience participation for this edition.

No 1 – Sporting Theme Tunes 👥

▶ Sporting Themes. Let me know your Top 3 Favourite Sporting TV Theme Tunes. Will your pick agree with our 'Esteemed' Panel?

No 2 – 10 Reasons Beer Piles on the Pounds 👥

▶ An Easy One – Why do we put weight on when we drink beer/alcohol? **Can we get to a list of 10?** I have 6. I'll start with an easy one. Beer itself is calorific.

Please see the Answers section at the back of the book.

Under the RADAR (Random Alert Detailing Alternative Reports)

Olympics and Para Are Now Nearly Over – Good Events for Team GB.

I did have a few bets on the Para Olympics.

Unfortunately, the bookies didn't agree with the commentator 'that they are all winners.' 😊

Did you see the wheelchair rugby? It was quite a spectacle.

https://www.bbc.co.uk/sport/disability-sport/58374295

Participant gets hit by a self-driving bus as he doesn't hear it …

https://www.independent.co.uk/asia/east-asia/paralympics-self-driving-bus-crash-injury-b1910475.html

And have you seen anything like it? … What a goal in the Para Soccer final!!!

https://www.mirror.co.uk/sport/other-sports/brazilian-blind-footballer-paralympics-goal-24910161

Covid Test Results Found discarded at BH Music Festivals – Are You Positive? Yes!!!!

https://www.dailymail.co.uk/news/article-9946547/Positive-Covid-test-strips-dumped-outside-Reading-Festival-site-attended-90K.html

Nitrous Oxide **(see (⌣|⌣) X3)** to be criminalised is no laughing matter…

https://www.getsurrey.co.uk/news/surrey-news/laughing-gas-nitrous-oxide-decriminalisation-13569178

Next Week's Issue

- More of the same crap jokes, unrelated events, and my making out that you lot are replying when you are clearly not!!!!!!!!!!!!!!

- Lena Returns – she weds, has a baby, goes on 'Staycation'???? Just like petrol or diesel, your gas is as good as mine. 😂

Next week's TV

None this week as a tellyban is now in place!!! My joke, so I'm using it again to claim it!!!

Stay safe,

Stevie

(‿|‿) **X1** Appeared in Private Eye this weekend but this SFTWS has been drafted for a week. I can prove it if it goes to court. Ian Heslop doesn't win (m)any, anyway!!!!!!!

(‿|‿) **X2** Unfortunately, Bazza was interrupted singing 'Can't smile without you,' but that wouldn't 'ave been (as) 'funny'!!!

(‿|‿) **X3** AKA Laughing Gas.

Issue No 34

Freedom Day Edition

Headlines:

▶ Rapid U-Turn by BJ, who Self-Isolates on Freedom Day!!!!

Leeds Utd Update - Leeds 3-1
WBA, 23rd May

Hi all ... CCC is attached for your pleasure when you see this sign. 😄

I hope you are well and not as heartbroken as me after the Euro 2020 Final. A great tournament, albeit a sad end!!! After early optimism and Sterling's value rising sharply, 😄 it all ended in a similar way.

My school/team mate and famous Leeds' footballer from Issue No 8 missed a penalty in a World Cup Shoot Out (sic). Does it help you guess who it is now?

Euro 2020 - Nearly Cancelled

I'm not sure if you missed the news as it was hardly reported, but the tournament was almost called off before the ¼ finals as the Ukrainian striker Chesti Ticklicough was diagnosed with Covid. 😄

Don't Mention the VAR!!!

I've been watching the England games in the pub and, would you believe it, saw the Germany game sat in the same seat I'd watched the 1996 Semi-Final almost 25 years earlier to the day!!! Where did that time go!!!?? I kept my seat from that day but did give one up on the bus the other day to a blind person, yet I lost my job. Not something I should do as a bus driver, I suppose. 😂

In the pub, however, it was not quite the same as 25 years ago. At seat service, much older clientele. Thank God, the only geriatric I saw was sitting next to me. 😂

At least we can use the old joke, for once, but the other way 'round.

What's the difference between Germany and a tea bag?

A tea bag stays in the cup longer.

Just for ol' times, revenge and reminiscing purposes (X😂X).

In this issue –

- ▶ Last Edition and Last Edition!!
- ▶ Freedom Day – July 19th Open with Care?!
- ▶ My Lockdown Beard – We've Been Hair Before!!
- ▶ My Daughter's Graduation
- ▶ Stevie's Puuuuuzzles (and Last Week's Answers) of the Week
  - » Quiz – Chickens or Dickens?

- Caption Comp is Back
- Under the RADAR – to Return Next Edition (if there is one)
- Lena Backwell – did she go too far!!!??
- Next week!!!!!!!!!!!!!!!!!! And, of course, lots of …
  (‿|‿)(‿|‿)(‿|‿)

Last Edition and Last Edition?!

As you know, I'm always keen to get feedback and a couple of days after my last issue, I got a response from Mr P of Guildersome, Leeds. 'I thought you were goin' to let me know tomorrow?' It took a while to register, but it did tickle me when it did (‿|‿) **X1.**

Last time, I also 'joked' about the edition being the last one … 'until the next one'!!! See also 'next week' below. Given, however, the recent announcement about 19th July (Freedom Day), etc., perhaps things ARE different/changing, but is it permanent as cases continue to soar?

As Winnie (‿|‿) **X2** once said …

- Now this is not the end. It is not even the beginning of the end. But it is, perhaps, the end of the beginning.

So, almost 1¼ years after my (full) 50th birthday and initial lockdown, **are we seeing a natural end to SFTWS as well?** 👥

Freedom Day – July 19th – Open with Care?!

Almost a year ago, we were also predicting something similar. So, be careful what you expect ...

Extract from No 12 - 'Another Lockdown Landmark (oops, don't say 'Landmark') tomorrow. Is this the end, or at least the beginning of the end?

https://www.gov.uk/government/speeches/foreign-secretarys-statement-on-coronavirus-covid-19-15-june-2020

I'm sure SFTWS will continue in some vane but **let me have your thoughts.** 👫

My Lockdown Beard – We've Been Hair Before!!

The beard has gone - banked into my shavings account with very little interest. 😬

Admittedly, not much of a beard given 16 months of growth (see before and after below). The first pic was in the pub last week watching the game, looking for a bit of British Bulldog spirit ...

The second, with daughter this week at Leeds Town Hall for her graduation (see next section).

To be fair, I didn't like having a beard, but it did eventually grow on me. 😏 I did come to have a certain affinity with it, and it is symbolic of who I am – it never grew up, either. 😄

With my daughter's graduation, I felt it was only right to 'get rid' of my beard, which I had been cultivating for so long, for the ceremony/photos.

So, I shaved it off. Just after I'd done it, I bumped into my daughter coming outta the bathroom. Her words were ... "Oh, okay, you look like a baby's bum. I thought you were just going to trim it." A bit late now. 😄

I did say if she graduated, I'd 'show my bum on the Town Hall steps!!' So, I suppose I did in a way (appropriate (‿|‿) **X3.**) Given I've been embarrassing her for so long, it also helped me to shave face a little. 😄

Daughter's Graduation

A strange affair that we could only see online. We met up later for throwing mortarboard' photos outside Town Hall, then proper 'professional' photos and a nice family meal.

As some are aware, Sammy graduated with honours in Concept and Digital Art and regularly provides drawings for SFTWS - see Caption Comp below. Again, perhaps this will be her last contribution, given she is starting to fulfil 'commissions,' regardless of SFTWS's future!!

🎵 Stevie's Puuuuuzzles
(and Last Week's Answers)
of the Week 🎵

» The Quiz - Chickens or Dickens

It's a strange way 'round this month. Usually, I pick the quiz based on the topics of discussion, but, given this might be the last one, I thought I might use 'My' (you do know my view on plagiarism?!) Chickens or Dickens Quiz. I was hoping to hold off 'til Xmas, but who knows if it will still be needed then?

To develop this quiz, I was reading "Great Expectations" by Charlie the other night. To be fair, it wasn't as good as I hoped it would be, and when I dropped it on my foot, it hurt like the Dickens (‿|‿) **X4.**

Anyway, a drink for the honest winner. To get you started, **Do you know what the bartender used to say to Charles in his day when he went for a tipple?**

Olive or Twist? 😄

'Hard Times' initially for Charlie D BUT helped by his Cider Business!!!

Finally, until Oliver Twist in 1837, his apple orchard

(really, Steve!?!) provided him with a much-needed source of income until he became popular. His cider was wanted by every girl. 😂 You work it out as this is a 'family show'!!! 👪

Quiz: Chickens or Dickens? 👪

 **or**

1. Brownlow
2. Australorp
3. Pecksniff
4. Bagnet
5. Barnevelder
6. Isa Brown
7. Swiveller
8. Orpington
9. Frazzle
10. Chuzzlewit
11. Leghorn
12. Pumblechook
13. Sebright
14. Buckeye
15. Bantam

Given might be the last issue, perhapsI should give you the answers. See the Answers section at the back of the book.

I genuinely have all his books (sic), inherited with the bookcase from my uncle (see the answer to Who's Who?).

Interestingly, when you do examine Dickens' works, there are some remarkable links with our experience over the last year and a bit.

Many of his books are linked to hardship, as we know, but there are many other comparisons, especially given how the pandemic has pitched/compared one nation or area against another (or tier, etc.). **Let me know if you can think of (m)any.**

Did you know "A Tale (Tier?!) of Two Cities" was originally published in two local newspapers?

It was the Bicester times; it was the Worcester times.

Finally, seriously, I suppose the one book that should reflect the times the best is 'Hard Times' but, actually, this was quite an unsympathetic approach to 'Utilitarianism' ($\smile | \smile$) **X5.** Surely, this is the debate we are starting to have now? Less of this seriousness, get back on with the crap jokes, Steve!!!!

Caption Competition

This was planned for the last issue, but I thought you'd had enough, so I held it over until now. Not as topical (or is it?), but surely, it's still worth a go!! Thanks to Sammy for her (last!!!!!) contribution.

Perhaps I've made it easy for you with an obvious one here, but this was a complete coincidence (‿|‿) **X6.**

No Under the RADAR this edition, but it is replaced by a **NEW Feature:**

'Turn of ESARHP'!!!

Seen/Heard recently –

- ▶ Relish Today, Ketchup tomorrow. Interpret for yourself. 🍔
- ▶ BJ – "a man who waits to see the way the crowd is running and then dashes in front and says, 'Follow me'." First said by Lord Heseltine years ago but IS he still getting away with it?
- ▶ People who act all intellectually superior by ending their thoughts with a Latin phrase

usually have no idea what they are doing, Et al.

► Is it me, or is the phrase 'due to' being used much more due to Covid?

► The phrase 'Bah humbug' has been heard a lot again recently! To finish with the Dickens theme, which has been covered elsewhere, see below.

The International Criminal Court of Justice in the Hague, in the case brought before it against the year 2020 and COVID-19, has ruled the phrase "Bah humbug!" is no longer just for Christmas and can now be used all year 'round.

Next Week's Issue/TV

► Next Edition
  » Let's see if it happens!!!
  » You decide – What do you want and in what format?
  » First trip for work on the train to Brum for 18 months

► TV
  » Memento – Wed 21st, BBC2 11.15 pm
  » Dunkirk – Fri 23rd, BBC4, 10 pm

All the best, and stay safe,

Stevie

(‿|‿) **X1** – Extract from the last issue - I've got something to tell you but can't atm!!! Sorry, sounds like one of those jokes I told when I was five years old!!!

How do you keep an idiot in suspense …

I'll tell you tomorrow. 😂

(‿|‿) **X2** – Winnie (Not Mandela – close but no cigar!!) Churchill from his 'Fight them on the Beaches' speech.

(‿|‿) **X3** – Sayings that are not used much anymore. If anything unlikely to happen was suggested, Grandad always used to say: *"If that happens, I'll show my bare bum on the town hall steps."* Some may also use Woolworths' window, etc.

(‿|‿) **X4** – Nothing to do with Charles, but "Dickens" in this context is a euphemism for "devil" as in, "What the Dickens!" It was a common expression centuries before Charles Dickens was born, having been used by Shakespeare in 'The Merry Wives of Windsor.' *Morris Dictionary of Word and Phrase Origins* by William and Mary Morris (HarperCollins, New York, 1977, 1988).

(‿|‿) **X5** What is utilitarianism theory?

Utilitarianism is a **theory** of morality. It advocates actions that foster happiness or pleasure and opposes actions that cause unhappiness or harm. "The greatest good for the greatest number" is a maxim of **utilitarianism**.

(⌣|⌣) **X6** Caption Comp. There may be a really obvious one here!!! Yet, that was/is a complete coincidence as this was 'drawn' a month ago, but I decided to give you a break and keep it back 'til this month!!!

(⌣|⌣) **X7 - The 15 Novels by Charles Dickens Listed by Publication Date**

The Pickwick Papers **– 1836**

The Pickwick Papers, also known as *The Posthumous Papers of the Pickwick Club*, was the first novel by Charles Dickens.

Chapman & Hall published it in monthly instalments from March of 1836 until November 1837.

Dickens worked a very serious subject into comedic Pickwick Papers - that of the injustice of the justice system.

Oliver Twist – **1837**

The second novel of Charles Dickens was *Oliver Twist*. The first edition had a longer title, *Oliver Twist; or, The Parish Boy's Progress*.

It was initially published in monthly instalments that began in February 1837 and ended in April 1839.

Dickens named the character Fagin after Bob Fagin, a fellow employee that young Charles Dickens met when he worked at a blacking factory.

Nicholas Nickleby – **1838**

The first instalment of Nicholas Nickleby was published on March 31, 1838, and the last instalment was published on October 1, 1839.

Dickens' mother, Elizabeth Dickens, was the model for the always-confused Mrs Nickleby. Luckily for Charles, she didn't recognise herself in the character. In fact, she asked someone if they "really believed there ever was such a woman."

The Old Curiosity Shop – **1840**

The Old Curiosity Shop was published in instalments in the periodical *Master Humphrey's Clock*. The first instalment was printed in April 1840, and the last was printed in February 1841.

Dickens was traumatised by the death of the book's character, Little Nell. As he was writing the novel, he felt as though he were experiencing the death of one of his children. It also brought back painful memories of the death of his sister-in-law, Mary Hogarth.

Barnaby Rudge – **1841**

Barnaby Rudge was published in instalments from February to November of 1841. It appeared in the magazine *Master Humphrey's Clock*.

The historical novel is set during the Gordon Riots of 1780.

Martin Chuzzlewit – **1843**

Martin Chuzzlewit was first published by Chapman & Hall in instalments that began in January 1843 and ran through to July 1844.

The novel was written after Dickens travelled to America in 1842. The trip left Dickens with a very unfavourable impression of the United States.

Dombey and Son – **1846**

Dombey and Son was first published in instalments that began in 1846 and ran through 1848.

Dickens gave a reading of the first instalment of Dombey to some of his friends. It went very well and gave Dickens the idea of doing public readings.

David Copperfield – **1849**

David Copperfield, Dickens' eighth novel, was first published as a serial. The first instalment was published in May 1849. The last instalment was issued in November 1850.

David Copperfield held a special place in Dickens' heart. In the preface to the 1867 edition, Dickens wrote, "like many fond parents, I have in my heart of hearts a favourite child. And his name is David Copperfield."

Bleak House – **1852**

Bleak House was published in instalments from March 1852 through September 1853.

This novel has the distinction of being perhaps the only work of classic literature featuring a character that dies by spontaneous combustion.

Hard Times – **1854**

The novel first appeared in Dickens' weekly periodical, *Household Words*. *Hard Times* was published in instalments that began in April of 1854 and ran through August of 1854.

Hard Times takes an unsympathetic look at utilitarianism. This no-nonsense movement relied heavily on statistics, rules and regulations.

Little Dorrit – **1855**

Little Dorrit was published in instalments from December 1855 through to June 1857.

The Marshalsea debtors' prison plays a large part in *Little Dorrit*. What very few people knew was that Dickens' father had been sent to Marshalsea for three months.

A Tale of Two Cities – **1859**

The first chapters of A Tale of Two Cities appeared in print in April 1859. The last chapter was printed in November of that same year.

A play, The Frozen Deep, was the inspiration for A Tale of Two Cities. Not only did the play give Dickens the idea for A Tale of Two Cities, but it also brought about lasting changes to Dickens' life in the form of Ellen Ternan.

Great Expectations – **1860**

Great Expectations was initially published in All the Year Round, a weekly periodical founded and owned by Charles Dickens. There were nine monthly instalments, running from December 1860 until August 1861.

In the novel, Pip, like Dickens himself, dreams of becoming a gentleman. However, Pip comes to realise that there is more to life than wealth and station.

Our Mutual Friend – **1864**

Our Mutual Friend is the last novel that Charles Dickens completed before his death.

An interesting feature of the novel is its focus on the "dust" business.

The Mystery of Edwin Drood – **1870**

The Mystery of Edwin Drood was the fifteenth novel

by Charles Dickens. Dickens was only halfway finished with the book when he died.

ISSUE NO 33
SUN 27TH JUNE 2021

Euros KO and Eurovision

Headlines:

- ▶ Hancock affair: PM has 'serious questions' to answer, says Labour
- ▶ Revealed: shocking scale of Twitter abuse targeting England at Euro 2020

Hi all … CCC is attached for your pleasure when you see this sign. 😌

A slight delay as I couldn't get it out last weekend … or the weekend before (I was tied up watching football!!!). BUT I'd better do it now as I need to move on to other stuff, of course. Door Matt (No More?) Hancock and England v Germany in particular.

You'll be glad to hear (?!) that it's a real bumper issue this month (as I just keep adding to it), in memory of my late uncle who would have been 82 in June and because this will be the **last issue** … until the next one!!!!!

The Euros kick off. England won (the first time in ten attempts they have won their first game in this tournament) and then drew against Scotland. Everything, however, was overshadowed by the incident in the Denmark/Finland game. Christian

Eriksen suffered a heart attack. He seems ok and has been discharged from the hospital.

In this Issue –

- ▶ Breaking News
- ▶ Mental Health Week
  - » It's Ok to Feel Weird
  - » Men are at Risk as We Don't Talk
- ▶ Euros and Eurovision – Football & Travel Chaos
- ▶ Attacks on Tech Giants to Clean Up or 'Silly Con Valet'!!
- ▶ PM in Secret Wedlock Down the Aisle
- ▶ Happiness for ALL/In No 10? No Short Cummings for the Govt?
- ▶ Friends Reunion
- ▶ Education Chaos – Levelling Up and Tutoring
  - » Music
  - » Sex Education
  - » Private Tutor
- ▶ Who's Who is Back!!
- ▶ ♫ Stevie's Puuuuuzzles of the Week!! ♫
- ▶ Under the RADAR (Random Alert Detailing Alternative Reports).
- ▶ Next Edition and Next Week's TV -
- ▶ (⌣|⌣)(⌣|⌣)(⌣|⌣) Inc. Lena is Back!!!

Breaking News

I've got something to tell you but can't atm!!! Sorry,

sounds like one of those jokes I told when I was five years old!!!

How do you keep an idiot in suspense ...

I'll tell you tomorrow 😄 OR

How do you confuse an idiot?

Put three spades in front of them and ask 'em to take their pick. 😄

Is it PC to say that these days, or is it idiotist!!!???

Unlocking of full lockdown is still in serious doubt (should know next month, now) as case numbers continue to rise as the Delta or 'Vindaflu' variant continues to take hold. Many are turning to the new punjab so they don't have to go sikh for a couple of days. 😄

Mental Health Week

Since the last issue, it's been Mental Health Week, so ...

How are you? As you know, it's not a rhetorical question as I don't do them ... What's the point? 😄

It is an important question.

» It's Ok to Feel Weird

When I DO get a reply to the above 'How are you?' question, it is often along the lines of ... 'I don't really know.' I think that's because, for the last 16 months, things have been very strange. So people felt ok to feel weird. BUT now, as we get back to 'normal,' people almost feel awkward saying they still don't feel quite right ... and probably won't for a long time. Let's face it, the old norm has gone, and who knows what the new norm will look like. I said on a Teams call the other day, 'Please raise your hand if you think the old norm will ever return.' For those who did, 'Please now (virtually) slap yourself with your raised hand.' 😂

» Men Are at Risk as We Don't Talk.

I do try to stay in touch and encourage others to do the same.

One of my mates has still not ventured out of his house again yet. I'm a little concerned about how 'big' he will be when he finally 'surfaces,' as every time I call him, night or day, he says, 'I'm just about to eat.' 😄 And to be fair, even before lockdown, he couldn't wear a belt and a tie at the same time as it turned him into sausages. 😄 So, it could be a 'Fire Brigade' job to get him out soon!!!! I think Lena mentions this phrase in her feedback letter, **see (‿|‿) X3,** but, given I'd already used it, I'm leaving it in!!!

▶ Next Issue's Health Message - The 'thing' men of a certain age should get checked. It's a digital test BUT does not involve an electronic device.

Euros and Eurovision

The Euros kick-off and England are through to face Germany. We won the first game (for the first time in ten attempts) and therefore got more points than we did in the Eurovision Song Contest!!! Weirdly, the system has been changed for Eurovision to ensure that this is supposed to be statistically impossible. Wrong!!!! We can't be that surprised, given we have been telling Europe to eff off for five years.

The good news is that Alexander Armstrong and Richard Osman have announced they are adding £250 to the pot. (‿|‿) X1.

Football

Finally, just to quickly 'close down' last season -

► Chelsea won the Champions League, and the Govt sent Penalty Notices to thousands of Man Utd/City fans for completely unnecessary trips to Europe.
► Brentford finally broke their play-off hoodoo (again, after their tenth time of asking) and were promoted to the Premier League. See also Under the RADAR.

Travel Chaos

Travel to and back from Europe in chaos. Yes, we

allowed fans to go to Portugal for the CL Final, but three days later, we reimposed the embargo. Thousands of 'holidayers' are left scurrying to get home or not sure if they should go in the first place. All travel guides in local libraries have now been moved to the horror section. 😩

Attacks (!!) on Tech Giants to Clean Up Act – or Is it Silly Con Valet? 😂

G7 try to agree to a tax on Big Tech. Nothing, apparently, is certain in life but death and taxes, yet 'tech' firms are working on a solution for the first (cryogenics) and ignoring the second!!! In addition, tech and robots continue to take lower-paid workers' jobs as the rich get richer. Without a meaningful tax, things are just going to get worse. Little Dishy Rishi is in full agreement on taxing these billionaires ... as long as this doesn't include his wife. 😂

Given the expense (and counting) of the pandemic and the 'catching up' agenda (see below), this tax could be the start of a real solution. Just like the non-binary prospector said when he saw the mountain range, "I bet there's gold in **them/their** hills." 😂

The above reminded me that my non-binary, Samurai joke (in the last edition) could have gone 'either way' 😂 and might have needed an explanation. So, I've given it another airing, **see** (‿|‿) **X2.** Like a bad Samurai swordsman, it might have gone over everyone's head initially!! Give it another go!!!!!???

If you still don't get it, the only comfort I can offer is …
their, their, their. 😔

PM in Secret Wedlock Down the Aisle

The Deputy PM, erm, I mean, Carrie Symonds, attempts
to make an honest man (good luck, there!!!) of the PM
in a secret ceremony at Westminster Cathedral. It did
look like the father of the bride marrying his daughter,
but hopefully, he will be there when she needs him
most and a better husband than PM.

Whenever my wife needs a bit of emotional support,
I let her colour in my black and white tattoos on my
upper arms – it always gives her a shoulder to crayon.
😔

The PM insisted on nobody wearing cravats with little
tear droplets on them and banned all his sobbing
oriental friends from attending the wedding. As we
know, he's not into emotional ties. 😔

Carrie immediately announced that they didn't want
any (more) kids. So, if anybody does, can they please
pick up BJ's hoard of 15+ asap? 😔

Happiness For All!? – well, for about 50% of the
population, anyway. You can work this one out or
wait for the X-rated version!!

The secret of a happy marriage may remain a bit of a
mystery, BUT apparently, scientists have discovered
the formulae for Happiness. See below …

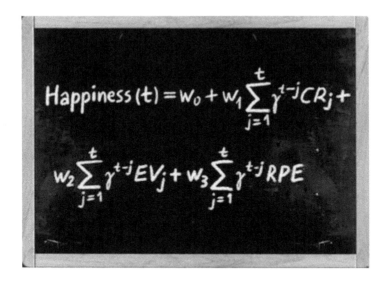

$$Happiness\,(t) = w_0 + w_1 \sum_{j=1}^{t} \gamma^{t-j} CR_j +$$

$$w_2 \sum_{j=1}^{t} \gamma^{t-j} EV_j + w_3 \sum_{j=1}^{t} \gamma^{t-j} RPE$$

Happiness in No 10? No Short Cummings for the Govt?

BJ hasn't discovered the formulae, though, to keep Dom Cum away, as he spent seven hours recently highlighting the, erm, shortcummings of the Govt approach to the pandemic at a Commons Select Committee. All would agree that Cummings is a completely unreliable witness, but most of what he said hit a chord with everything we've experienced over the last 16 months.

One of the things Cummings said, is that a (political) system must be broken if it ends with a choice between Corbyn and Johnson. So, might he have a point there at least?! As we know, Capitalism is struggling, but Communism doesn't work. **So, what do we do?**

Did you know that the writer of the communist manifesto, Karl Marx, is the brother of the less well-known Irish Onya, who actually invented the starting pistol? His brother, Skid, invented Vanish the stain remover. 😄. Or should I have said hiS(kid) brother?

And perhaps appropriately, it was **Groucho Marx** who said, "The secret of life is honesty and fair dealing. If you can fake that, you've got it made." Sounds about right atm with the political situation. He also said, 'pints, gallons and litres.' Speaks volumes in these times as well. 😄

Mr J(ohnson) was bard from working on his Shakespeare novel to ensure he attended Cobra/CV-19 meetings!! Perhaps the book should be entitled 'The Shaming of the True.' 😄

Friends Reunion

Friends and marriage must be in the Happiness formulae somewhere. It was the Friends TV sitcom reunion recently (see below) that was watched by zillions!!! I do have the box set on a shelf in my bedroom, but I much prefer to read my music mags these days. So, I keep them under my bed as I like to keep my Friends close but my NMEs closer. 😄

Everybody looks older in Friends except the baby twins, of course … who still look exactly the same. 😄

https://www.mediamole.co.uk/entertainment/tv-ratings/news/friends-reunion-episode-draws-1point7-

million-in-uk_449327.html

Education Chaos – Levelling Up and Tutoring

Education is Important BUT Levelling Up is apparently NOT as Importanter. 😄

School 'Catch Up' Tsar resigns after money is inadequate to redress the balance caused by CV-19. I thought I'd highlight some aspects. **This Edition, Tutoring.**

Music –

A tutor who tooted the flute,
Tried to tutor two tooters to toot.
Said the two to the tutor:
"Is it harder to toot or
To tutor two tooters to toot?"

Sex Education – will this be addressed as a core subject?
If they do, will they have to get extra people in to teach kids about sex education? If so, would it be a prostitutor? 😄
Private Tutor – and not just someone who doesn't fart in public. 😄
When I was young, I had a private tutor for my spelling. I had to get rid of him eventually as he just criticised everything I did all the time. Looking over my shoulder, he would make that noise with his tongue behind his teeth. Tuht tuht this, tuht

tuht that, non-stop all the time. Turns out my spelling was worse than I thought; I'd ordered a private tutter instead. 😂

Who's Who is Back! Name the Person

As before, I will give you a few clues to a person's identity. **Please have a go and see if you can name him or her.** 👫

Here We Go ...

After a fall a few years ago, this person ended up in A&E. After waiting all night, having x-rays, etc., this person was finally being checked over by a doctor before being admitted. So, after being in A&E all night, the nurse needed to do the 'Alzheimer's test.'

Question 1 – 'Can you tell me the queen's full title/name?' asked the doctor.

'Which queen? The current queen, Queen Elizabeth the second, Queen Boadicea ...? Which?' was the reply.

'Okay, that's fine,' said the doctor and continued ...
Question 2 – 'Can you tell me when the first World War started?'

'I assume you mean the Great War ... but it wasn't known as World War I until the second World War occurred. It started in 1914, don't you want to know when it ended, etc.?'

'That's fine,' the doc said again ... smiling and very

amused by now. And continued…

'Finally, I'm going to mention an address to you, and I want you to remember it as I'm going to ask you again about it later. The address is West End Rise, Leeds 17.'

Response – 'Do you really want me to remember that one? It's the same address you asked me to remember when I was in here after my last fall nearly two years ago.'

'Yes', said the doctor, 'we do tend to use the same address. You might be shocked and all that, BUT there's obviously nothing wrong with your memory.'

See the Answers section at the back of the book.

♫ Stevie's Puuuuuzzles
(and Last Week's Answers)
of the Week ♫

This is a speed test. If you 'try' it as a group, give 10 points for whoever finishes first, 9 for second place, etc., as well as the points for each correct answer. If you do it on your own, then give yourself 10 points for under a minute, 9 for 1 min 30, etc.

1. You have to take a tablet every ½ hour … How long does it take to take three tablets?
2. How many animals of each species did Moses take aboard the Ark?
3. How many months of the year have 28 days?

4.   You are in a square house, and every wall faces south … you come out of the door and see a bear … what colour is it?

5.   A farmer has 17 sheep, and all but nine die … how many are left?

6.   You are driving a bus from Inverness to Newquay. The first stop is Newcastle and picks up 2 customers, then stop at Leeds and pick up a mother with her two sons. Then final stop at Birmingham and pick up two adults. What is the name of the bus driver?

7.   You are taking part in a race. You overtake the second person. What position are you in?

8.   If you overtake the last person, then you are … ?

9.   Take 1000 and add 40 to it. Now add another 1000. Now add 30. Add another 1000. Now add 20. Now, add another 1000. Now add 10. What is the total?

10. Mary's father has five daughters: 1. Nana, 2. Nene, 3. Nini and 4. Nono. What is the name of the 5th daughter?

Let me know how you get on 👣 … A prize for the best (honest) score. Please see the Answers section to check your results.

Under the RADAR (Random Alert Detailing Alternative Reports). Stories you may have missed (and mostly linked to above)

Eurovision nil points

https://www.manchestereveningnews.co.uk/news/
tv/eurovision-fans-says-netflix-predicted-20659694

Brentford and chairman

https://www.facebook.com/
watch/?v=821988105401923

William Shakespeare dies. Not All Well That Ends
Well....in this case!!!

https://www.bbc.co.uk/news/uk-england-coventry-
warwickshire-57234741

Middle East Issue Netanyahu set to lose power.

https://www.bbc.co.uk/news/world-middle-
east-57396990

I do like to give all my post addressed to the 'Occupier'
to my next-door Israeli neighbour. 😄

'Horror' Crash on Motorway

https://www.standard.co.uk/news/uk/
cambridgeshire-a14-crash-tomato-puree-
spill-b938432.html

Spiderman meme

https://inews.co.uk/news/politics/spiderman-meme-
explained-meaning-pointing-dominic-cummings-
evidence-select-committee-1020424

Next Edition/TV
- ▶ Next week

Green Shoots for Gardening as Allotments in the pandemic take off ('sprouts')!! We ask a gardener what ARE the other uses of multi-purpose compost? 😄

▶ TV

- His Girl Friday, Film 4, 11 am, Monday 28th
- Casablanca, BBC4,10.40 pm Thursday 1st

'See ya' soon. Stay safe and take care …

All the best,

Stevie

(‿|‿) **X1** Pointless, the game show on TV, adds to the jackpot every time there is a pointless score!!

(‿|‿) **X2** Extract from the last issue ... Line of Duty (LOD) does try to be as PC and on the beat as possible with diversity, minorities in key roles, etc. In Series 7, apparently, they are going to have a non-binary Samurai swordsman as the main killer. But HOW do you think they will kill their victims? I suspect ... **'They slash them.'**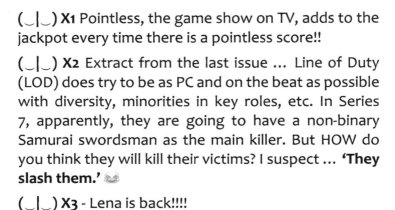

(‿|‿) **X3** - Lena is back!!!!

As we move slowly out of the pandemic, here are Lena's thoughts on the legacy of COVID-19.

Dear Steve,

I can't wait to get back to work in an office, but I fear that so-called "working" from home is going to continue as a legacy - with devastating consequences for business efficiency, the national economy and my mental health.

Isn't it ironic that chubby folk are at high risk from the virus, but the legacy of Covid is a UK pandemic of obesity because so many are "working" from home, hardly moving, overdosing on daytime TV and eating biscuits all day?

Take my husband (well, I wish someone would). He's not worn trousers for 15 months because now only trackies will fit around his massive thighs. He can't wash properly because he can't waddle his way up the stairs anymore, which is a relief for me, Steve, I can tell you. He's huge! His arteries flow like hosepipes full of custard. Fatbergs have healthier complexions, and the only exercise he gets is walking to the fridge. If he ever does need to go out of the house, it'll be a fire brigade job.

I'm sure he's not the only Fatberg-sized home-worker stuck nervously in his bedroom gorging on Waggon Wheels and Cash in the Attic. So, I've got to ask – when's the office going to be open, Steve??

The other legacy will be divorce. Post lockdown, there are a lot of unsatisfied, lonely women out there. Gorgeous, lonely women in their prime, Steve. Women, Steve, who have come to realise the profound shortcomings of the idiots they got locked down with for 15 intolerable months. And yes, I am certainly regretting that ill-advised night in the Utopia nightclub that rounded off the CSSC trip to London in 1996, which you organised.

Finally, we all know that hindsight is a wonderful thing. But it would have helped many of us during lockdown if someone had produced an amusing newsletter to keep us connected and lift our spirits. You know the kind of thing, Steve, a newsletter with jokes that are funny and stories that readers could understand and which raise a smile without needing a CCC prompt to spot the punchline. If only someone amongst us had put a newsletter like that together, Steve.

Oh well, there's bound to be another pandemic along soon. My husband has probably eaten a few bats amongst the snacks he's devoured while watching Tipping Point this afternoon.

When he should have been working.

That's it for now,

Bye-eeeeeeee!!! XX @@!!

Yours truly

Lena Backwell

ISSUE NO 32
THURS 13TH MAY 2021

Daughter Mel's Special
26th Birthday Edition

Headlines:

- ▶ Boris Johnson is under fire for delaying Covid public inquiry until 2022
- ▶ 'There is no safe place in Gaza': Israeli strikes terrify inhabitants

Leeds Utd Update - Leeds 3-1 Spurs, Sat 8th May (and we get blathered watching it in pub!!!)

Hi all ... CCC is attached for your pleasure when you see this sign. 😄

My daughter was 26 last week. So, another year flies by!!! Issue No. 6 is last year's edition which was in 'honour' of her 25th birthday. Obviously!!!

In This Edition -

- ▶ Football. Sleaze, Sleaze, Sleaze!!!!
- ▶ Curtains for the PM?!!
- ▶ Line of Duty (LOD) Burner Phones and Organised Crime
- ▶ Ryan Giggs – Running Down D(a) Wing!!!!!
- ▶ Prince Phillip I (PPI)
- ▶ Post Office (PO) – PO Told to PO!!

- ► Stevie's Puuuuuzzles of the Week and Line of Duty (LOD) and Blue Peter Post Office Quiz
- ► Next Edition TV

I'm back! Sorry for the delay for some, but I have less time now pubs are open (you'll be glad to hear). As we know, the pubs are due to be open inside from next week, so more on that next time. I better send this out tonight; otherwise, it'll end up as long as the dead sea scrolls!!

Sad News - Farewell David Grant!!!!!

Some sad news. David G has sadly passed away. Who is going to respond (and contribute) to my emails/ newsletter now?! So, he will never fulfil his dream of starting his chicken dating business. He tried many times but just couldn't make hens meet. 😂 One of his faves (and, to be fair, mine too).

Whenever I used to 'bump' into him, he would often repeat this 'joke.' I can remember the first time I told it to him in the Black Horse, Otley, approximately eight years ago. The same night he told me, 'I've quit working at the Cat Protection Centre, Steve, as they've reduced meowers.' 😂 Just returning the favour as that was one of his (jokes) and one of my faves!!!

Football

Since the last issue, amazing results for Leeds against some of the so-called 'Super 6' culminating in a win against Spurs. So, with the Super League in tatters (that can't be said for BJ's curtains) and his refurb making the headlines (or not!!!), we have moved from Leeds, Leeds, Leeds … to … Sleaze, Sleaze, Sleaze. 😂

Curtains for Boris? Not Based on Bi/Local Election Results

To be fair, without Venetian Blinds, it would be curtains for everyone. 😂 There are many issues over Johnson getting his mates (Curt and Rod) to sort out his décor, but he's hoping to draw a close to this soon. A shot in the arm for BJ is the success of the vaccine rollout as it's the only show in town atm and the only thing anyone seems to care about.

'It's the Blind Man.' I can't resist one of my fave jokes (with only a little relevance) recreated on Vicar of Dibley (was it the first ever episode?) many years ago …

https://www.youtube.com/watch?v=ljMo77coDrk 😂

BJ and the Bear (Face Liar? As Ted on LOD would say) … (⌣|⌣) X1

Can I be serious for a moment?

'I don't know. Can you, Steve?'

The jury is out on whether the refurbishment issue is 'cutting through' atm with the public. Last week's elections would suggest not. But I'd like to offer a comparison with something that certainly is … Line of Duty (LOD)!!! Series 6 concluded (for now?) recently.

- ► Sofa(r) So Good for PM, BUT is it a slow Burner?!

This, of course, is NOT about refurbishment and curtains but about who pays for what and transparency. Is our most important politician being influenced by ('in the pocket of') others? Just like in LOD, nobody is saying he is being bribed, but rules on lobbying need addressing immediately as it's a shambles and has been getting worse for many years. In addition, given that his mobile number has been in general circulation for 15 years ... has he got a couple of 'Burner' (‿|‿) **X2** phones on the go? 😬

Any more comparisons or differences between LOD and BJ/Govt? 🐱

I'll think of some!!!!

Line of Duty Series 7?

Surely there will be a Series 7 after the anti-climax of the last episode? The search goes on for the 4th Man/'H,' but potentially, in Series 7, Ted (Hastings) will be looking for a man with one eye.

If he doesn't find him, he's going to look for him with both eyes. 😂

LOD does try to be as PC and on the beat as possible with diversity and minorities in key roles, etc. In Series 7, apparently, they are going to have a non-binary Samurai swordsman as the main killer. But HOW do you think they will kill their victims? I suspect ... 'They slash them.' 😁 If you still don't 'get it, **see (⌣|⌣) X3.**

Anyway, an official police spokesman said, 'If anybody says that the police are as corrupt as this in real life, they can kiss my Rolex' 😁. In the next issue, a policeman refuses to accept a vagrant urinating on his wrist. 'Not on my watch,' he declares. 😁

I'm not sure if ever told you, but I was once chased by a police dog. To try and get away, I went through a tunnel, over a little see-saw and then jumped through a hoop of fire. It didn't work; the dog seemed to know my every move. 😁

My First Job for the Mafia

Many might not know this as well, but my first procurement job was to supply Filofaxes to the Mafia. I was involved in very organised crime. 😁

It's Not Just About 'Finding Bent Coppers,' (as Ted would say) BUT White and Wong!!!!

Two men worked on the same police force. One was named Michael White and the other Kevin Wong. Together, they formed a good-cop-bad-cop team known as White and Wong.

When White was killed in the line of duty, Wong's brother joined the force, but it was never quite the same. After all, two Wongs don't make a White. 😁

Prince Phillip 1st (PPI)

Farewell to Prince Phillip the 1st - he must have got

his PPI when he married the Queen. 😄 The only man I know named after a playing field and a Community Centre. 😄 (‿|‿) X4.

Reports came in just after he died that he had died peacefully in the Queen's arms. Bloody typical that even before pubs reopened properly, he was in the pub. 😄 One rule for one and, etc.

Seriously, he was a dedicated public servant. The worst thing is the people who 'slagged' him off for years and then said what a wonderful bloke he was after he died. He is just another person of many (along with DG) who have been sadly lost.

Ryan Giggs, Ryan Giggs … Running Down D(e) Wing

In the news recently, an unnamed (oops) ex-footballer has been charged with assault. Given that he is living in Manchester (for now), he does Miss Wales occasionally. 😄 Since he has stopped playing football, however, he also does Miss Training as well. 😄 If he gets banged up, then it won't be just Liverpool Party goers doing Giggs (‿|‿) X5. 😄 It might also be a reshowing of that alternative film title for Saving Private Ryan (you work it out) that is (re)released before he is.

Post Office (PO) is told to PO in Unmitigated Disaster

It's not just me with awful delivery, but the PO is in chaos recently and, for once, not in the 'delivery' area … https://www.bbc.co.uk/news/business-56718036.

Finally, many of the convictions have been quashed.

Who'd have thought it of the PO? BUT the devil can take many forms. Which is why you never wanna be behind him in the PO queue. 😄

As we know, the Post Office has been mis-delivering for years … and it should have been properly addressed. 😄

I was delighted when the postman finally delivered the book I ordered the other day, 'How to Make Your Own Watch.' It's about time. 😄

🎵 Stevie's Puuuuuzzles of the Week 🎵💥

Relevant as always …

LOD – https://www.joe.ie/movies-tv/the-hardest-line-of-duty-quiz-youll-ever-take-692344

Post Office – https://www.bbc.co.uk/cbbc/quizzes/blue-peter-letters-mail-post-fact-quiz Go to the link and press start for the Blue Peter PO Quiz.

Others (Top Up) –

- ▶ What goes around the world but stays in one corner?
- ▶ What two words have the most letters?
- ▶ What word begins with and ends in 'n' and means constipation?

See the Answers section at the back of the book.

Under the RADAR (Random Alert Detailing Alternative Reports).

Stories you may have missed:

Colin the Caterpillar gets Scottish chippy treatment https://www.bbc.co.uk/news/uk-scotland-glasgow-west-56955873

John Lewis advert ... almost for everyone... https://www.independent.co.uk/news/uk/home-news/boris-johnson-john-lewis-furniture-b1839206.html

Clubbers return to Liverpool. https://www.bbc.co.uk/news/newsbeat-56943652

Next Edition/TV

- ► TV – Snooker Gods (continues) – BBC2 Sundays and iPlayer

'See ya' soon. Stay safe and take care ...

Steve

(‿|‿) **X1** https://en.wikipedia.org/wiki/B._J._and_the_Bear

(‿|‿) **X2** https://www.urbandictionary.com/define.php?term=Burner%20phone

(‿|‿) **X3 Pronouns** are words used to refer to people (for example, she/**her**, he/him, or **they/them). OR THEY SLASH THEM.** An easy way to normalise the use of **pronouns** is to **include** them in your **email signature**. … Having **pronouns** in an **email signature** signals you as an LGBTQIA+ ally.

(‿|‿) **X4** https://www.theguardian.com/leeds/2011/apr/12/leeds-prince-philip-centre-phab-club Where I grew up and the field I played many a footy game on!!!!!

(‿|‿) **X5** https://www.youtube.com/watch?v=QQd2GX-V7XY

Issues are now in chronological order from March 2020

ISSUE NO 1
23RD MARCH 2020

Lockdown Day and
My 50th (!!) Birthday

Headlines:

▶ UK could face Italy-style lockdown, warns Boris Johnson

Leeds Utd Update - Leeds 2-0
Huddersfield, 7th March

And the last time our local Super 6 was won ... by ME!!!!!!!!!!

Hi,

Today's diary/thoughts just in case you get too bored. Apologies, but opting out by typing STOP is not available at present!!!

The rambling northern madman is back!

How are you? Not a rhetorical question as I've given up asking them ... What's the point?

Realising you are probably missing me??? I didn't want you to get withdrawal symptoms!!!

Remember, at times like this, there is always someone worse off than you. Perhaps, JUST be grateful you are not me. Remember, I spend 24 hours a day with 'me' every day!!!!

In fact, when someone said to me this morning ... 'What have you been doing with yourself?' I said, 'To be fair, everything. Whatever I'm doing, I'm always there and doing it wiv misen. Went for a jog; I was there. Had a shower; I was there ...' etc. ...

'Joke/story' of the day ... Something relevant, perhaps?

I was going to leave this email ... 'bad joke'-free, but then I had a brain transplant ... and changed my mind!! 😄 (Symbol retrospectively inserted as it didn't happen in the first few editions.)

Last Night's NHS 'Clap'

I don't have much involvement with my neighbours atm, and last night was the first time I've seen them for ages (for the 'clap,' so to speak).

I recently ordered a book called ... 'How to Have Nothing to Do with Your Neighbours.' Unfortunately, it was delivered whilst I was out. 😄

Other things ...

Films on today (if you have access) that are worth watching or 'taping' for the weekend -

- ▶ Kill Bill 9 pm Sony pictures

- ► Rocketman 8 pm Sky premiere tonight and tomorrow, etc
- ► Witness 10.45 pm BBC1

Today's Word of the Day

Not a bad word to start with and to 'live'/consider ...

cordial

adjective | KOR-jul

Definition

1 a: showing or marked by warm and often hearty friendliness, favour, or approval : politely pleasant and friendly

   b: sincerely or deeply felt

2: tending to revive, cheer, or invigorate

Coming soon: Stevie's Crap Joke Bingo?!

Usually, I look forward to Friday, but tomorrow is just more of the same ... hey ho!!!

Stay safe and strong.

Stevie

Issue No 2

Friday 3rd April 2020

2nd *Week of Clapping for the NHS*

Headlines:

- ▶ Spain records first fall in daily death toll in four days as French police mobilise
- ▶ Britain opens new hospital as peak predicted earlier than anticipated
- ▶ Cases climb above 1 million as deaths pass 53,000

Hi,

Another week ... hopefully SFTWS will provide a little light relief for all.

Here we are again at Friday ... is that only a week?! **WOW!!!** I hope you all clapped last night.

My Neighbours ...

Once again, the 'clap' gave me a chance to see my neighbours.

On one side, my neighbour stopped to clap, but he had been mowing his lawn. He was hunched over his mower. He said ... 'Like us all, I'm just going through a rough patch.'

I told him he could use my lawnmower at any time he wanted ... as long as it never left my garden!!!!

On the other side, my neighbours ... a couple, have just produced a sex tape ... although they don't know it yet!! 😬

On the other side, 😬 my neighbours came round last night at two in the morning last night and started banging on my door. Luckily, I was still up, playing my bagpipes. 😬

On the other side!!!!!!

Finally, on 'neighbours,' I think it was Quentin Crisp who once said, 'Health consists of having the same disease as one's neighbours.' ... How apt is this now?

I also like the one ... 'The only people who hear both sides of a family argument are the next-door neighbours'!!!!! No idea who said that.

This Week's Quiz x2

Please see the end of this issue for probably the best 2 quizzes of the week so far (if you haven't already seen them). The first one is good for both kids and adults alike. The second one is 30 songs from the '80s. The answers will be in the next issue.

Myth-buster ... SPAM and Dogs

Stevie's Myth-busting Moment of the Week. Obviously, recent emails suggesting chopped pork and ham is a way to get COVID-19 were wrong. Please ignore; it's just Spam!!! 😬

Authorities have announced dogs are now being

released from quarantine as it has been confirmed they cannot pass on COVID-19 ... W.H.O. let the dogs out??!! 🐶

This is a feeble attempt at a joke from earlier in the week ... and yet yesterday, there was actually a story that said cats could pass on COVID-19 ...

https://www.theguardian.com/world/2020/apr/01/cats-can-infect-each-other-with-coronavirus-chinese-study-finds

Another small positive is that the BBC are using Ali P again to reinforce the need for a routine. See below. Classic clip - Ahaaaaaaa... Bondathon!

https://www.campaignlive.co.uk/article/bbc-recruits-alan-partridge-miranda-stay-home-films/1678450

Word of the Day/Week ... see the end of this issue.

Film of the Day/Week ... The Changeling ITV3 Tonight.

Next Week!!!

Next week is Easter, and I will be interviewing Arnold Schwarzenegger (one of the biggest names in Hollywood ... 20 letters!!) on -

- ▶ His favourite Christian festival,
  - Attending fancy dress parties as his fave composer ... and much more!!!!!!!

Go on, you know them!!!

If you want to join us, we'll be at the Cottage Road Cinema, Row P (the very poor seats!!!), Aisle B, Back!!!

Next Week's Challenge ...

A chance to have a sweep/virtual bet (remember them?!) as I'm going to time how long it takes me to go on my regular jog. I hate it, but I'm continuing ... 'How slow can I go!!!!!?????? How slow can I go???!!!'

Finally, see below my 'recently penned' (not) poem that I'd like to share with you all.

Byeeeeeeeeeeeeeeeeeeeeeeeeeee for now.

Stevie

The Rainbow Children

The history books will talk of now,
That time the world stood still.
When every family stayed at home,
Waved out from windowsills-
At those they loved but could not hold,
Because they loved them so.
Yet, whilst they did they noticed all the flowers start
to grow.

The sun came out, they can recall,
And windows, rainbows filled.
They kicked a football in their yards,
Until the night drew in.
They walked each day but not too close,
That time the world stood still.
When people walked straight down the roads,
That once the cars did fill.

They saw that people became ill,
They knew the world was scared.
But whilst the world stood still they saw,
How much the whole world cared.
They clapped on Thursdays from their doors,
They cheered for the brave.
For people who would risk their lives,

115

So others could be saved.

The schools closed down, they missed their friends,
They missed their teachers so.
Their mams and dads helped with their work,
They helped their minds to grow.
The parents used to worry that,
As schools were put on hold,
Their children wouldn't have the tools,
They'd need as they grew old.

But history books will talk of them,
Now adults, fully grown.
Those little boys and girls back then,
The ones who stayed at home.
They'll tell you that they fixed this world,
Of all they would fulfil.
The RAINBOW children building dreams,
They'd dreamed whilst time stood still 🌈

God bless you all ... all our children are bright rainbows
to me and always will be. Keep building dreams,
praying hard and keeping safe. A little OTT, perhaps,
but left in with the photo ... see end for disclaimer ...

PS ... Obviously, I nicked the poem from someone but you do know my views on plagiarism!!!!!??? If not, that's another thing for next week.

Quiz 1: TV/Films Blocks – Name the TV show or film from the block-shaped characters.

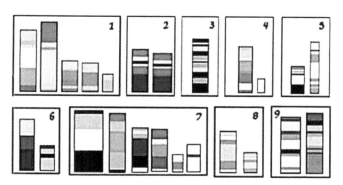

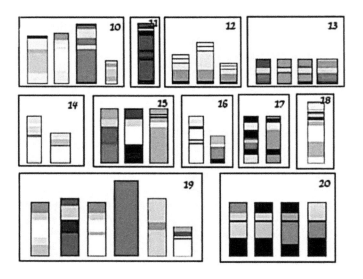

Word of the Week

cocoon

verb | kuh-KOON

Definition

: to wrap or envelop in or as if in a cocoon

Did You Know?

Since at least the late 1600s, English speakers have been using the noun cocoon for the silky covering that surrounds a caterpillar or other insect larva in the pupa stage of metamorphosis. The word derives, via French *cocon*, from Occitan *coucoun*, which, in turn, emerged from coco, an Occitan term for "shell." Linguists believe the Occitan term was probably born of the Latin word *coccum*, a noun that has been translated as *kermes*, which refers to the dried bodies of some insects that are sometimes found on certain trees. The verb cocoon has been with us since the latter half of the 19th century.

Examples of COCOON

Lily got out of the water and *cocooned* herself in a large beach blanket.

"By the time the United States entered World War I, France and England had been battling the Germans, the Turks and the Austro-Hungarians for nearly four years... America, cocooned by great oceans, saw the struggle as distant and obscene." Wayne Washington, *The Palm Beach (Florida) Post*, 23 Jan 2020

Quiz No. 2 – 30 Songs from the 80s

Issue No 3

Shopping Scarcity Easing?

Headlines:

▶ Raab suggests the UK lockdown could last at least another month

Hi,

SFTWS becomes SFTWS ... i.e. Something for the Weekend, Sir, becomes Something for the Week, Sir!!!!! As it will give me chance to draft over the weekend.

Another week over. How are you? What do you get when you cross a joke with a rhetorical question? ... 😄

Lockdown is now becoming tedious. It's like my first ever job, drilling holes for water - it was well-boring!!!! 😄 More on my previous jobs in next week's issue, perhaps!! And a vicious rumour about the future - I might actually start doing some proper work for my current employee, Highways England!! Don't get your hopes up, Boss!!!!

Shopping Easier?

At least, it appears that the shopping scarcity is less acute. Although I'm still struggling to get paella, rice, tequila and a sombrero (to flatten it, perhaps, as in the Covid curve!!!!) ... 'Hispanic buying,' mi thinks??!!

Arnie Interview!!!!

This issue is a little late this week, but I had to wait until my interview with Arnie (Schwarzenegger) was over.

Just in case you didn't know what to expect (or didn't even get to the end of last week's edition), his answers were predictable.

When asked, 'What is your favourite Christian festival?' he said, 'You have to love Easter, baby.'

When choosing an outfit for going to a composers' fancy dress party, he said, 'I'll be Bach'!!

Keep Safe ... Physically and Mentally

Bad news over the weekend as someone stole my antidepressants. Whoever they are, I hope they're happy!!

Seriously, please be careful because people are going crazy from being in lockdown!

I've just been talking about this with the microwave and toaster (over a coffee), and we all agreed that things are getting bad.

I didn't mention anything to the washing machine as she puts a different spin on everything.

Certainly not to the fridge either, as he is acting cold and distant.

In the end, the iron straightened me out as she says everything will be fine; no situation is too pressing.

The vacuum was very unsympathetic ... told me to just suck it up, but the fan was more optimistic and hoped it would all soon blow over!

The toilet looked a bit flushed when I asked its opinion and didn't say anything, but the doorknob told me to get a grip. 😁

The front door said I was unhinged and the curtains told me to ... yes, you guessed it 😆... pull myself together. 😅

😂 **Maybe a chance to come up with more?** E.g. the garden says it's a jungle out there!!

Films/TV of the week

The Vikings ... Wed BBC2.

Killing Eve ... Returns with Season 3 next Sunday, but you can get the first episode from tonight on iPlayer.

And, Finally ...

I've actually removed a panel in my fence so I can have a beer in the sun with my neighbour (you knew I would get them in somewhere). Please note no ?????? or !!!!!!This is not my usual feeble attempt at a joke.

And, Finally x2 ...

If you are an extrovert and need tips on 'social distancing' ... Why don't you ask an introvert? They've been doing it for years!!!!! 😄

Any requests … other than 'STOP'?

And, Finally x3 … Last Week's Quiz answers

Quiz 1 - TV 'BLOCK' ANSWERS
1. The Simpsons
2. Super Mario Bros
3. Batman
4. Tin Tin & Snowy
5. Dexter's Laboratory
6. Wallace & Gromit
7. Family Guy
8. Tom & Jerry
9. Toy Story
10. Flintstones
11. Deadpool
12. Despicable Me
13. South Park
14. Pinky & The Brain
15. Futurama
16. Danger Mouse
17. Mickey & Minnie Mouse
18. Bugs Bunny
19. Star Wars
20. Star Trek

Quiz 2 - 30 Songs from the 80s
1. 99 Red Balloons - Nena
2. Eye Of The Tiger - Survivor

3. Jump - Van Halen
4. Sledgehammer - Peter Gabriel
5. Died In Your Arms - Cutting Crew
6. Africa - Toto
7. When Doves Cry - Prince
8. Video Killed The Radio Star - The Buggles
9. Livin' On A Prayer - Bon Jovi
10. Walk Like An Egyptian - The Bangles
11. Sweet Dreams - Eurythmics
12. Walking On Sunshine - Katrina & The Waves
13. Stonehenge - Spinal Tap
14. Another One Bites The Dust - Queen
15. Heaven Is A Place On Earth - Belinda Carlisle
16. Gold - Spandau Ballet
17. Romeo And Juliet - Dire Straits
18. Blue Monday - New Order
19. Road To Nowhere - Talking Heads
20. Ghost Town - The Specials
21. Super Trooper - Abba
22. It's A Kind Of Magic - Queen
23. Monkey Gone To Heaven - Pixies
24. Total Eclipse Of The Heart - Bonnie Tyler
25. Ashes To Ashes - David Bowie
26. I Saw The Whole Of The Moon - The Waterboys
27. She Bangs The Drums - Stone Roses
28. Danger Zone - Kenny Loggins
29. You Spin Me Right Round - Dead Or Alive
30. Higher Love - Steve Winwood

Next Week

A tour around the world to see how they are coping.

See ya …

Stay safe and healthy.

Cheers.

Stevie

Issue No 4

RIP Leeds' Legend
Norman Hunter Edition

Headlines:

- ▶ Trump warns China over outbreak
- ▶ Global death toll passes 160,000 and 40,000 UK deaths now 'Feasible'
- ▶ China reports its lowest daily cases for a month

Hi,

Are you ok? (yes, 'you'!!!) 👬 As I said, not rhetorical.

This week's edition is a little later than planned. Apologies for that.

My northern madman ramblings are becoming quite long, so I've come up with three ways to shorten this issue:

- ▶ Joke/Question or punchline/answer ONLY … and much more Audience Participation 👬 (see below) for the rest.
- ▶ Delete 'loads'
- ▶ (and next week) I'm going to tear the newsletter in half!!!!

That Was The Week That Was (TWTWTW)

Sad news!!!! Norman Hunter was born 29 October

1943; died 17 April 2020

Unfortunately, I start to write this with some sad news. Norman Hunter, the Leeds Legend, who lived in Horsforth, Leeds (not far from me), has sadly passed away along with many others this week and the thousands already. A 50/50 battle that Norman couldn't win. RIP Norman.

On that note, please look at a very well-deserving cause below and ignore the rest of this edition if you wish. I know you probably do that, anyway?! NHS charity is very dear to our hearts with a significant local presence in Leeds. PPE is a crisis within a crisis that is NOT going away (as promised by many), so please help.

https://www.justgiving.com/crowdfunding/ schoolofsew?utm

Anyway, as the crow once said to me ... Caw Caw Caw Caw. It's Just For (a) Good Cause!!! 😄

Breaking News. I'm sending some of the money I'm saving on beer. Now that should keep the NHS going for a bit!

How things change from just a few weeks ago!!!

Do you recall a few short weeks ago, there was talk that Covid could cost 20 thousand UK deaths? At the time, most thought that seemed ludicrous and just 'managing expectations' ... and yet this week, the announcement of 40,000 seems quite plausible.

The PUB ... remember that?

Anyway, some good news this week (for me, anyway), I got to go to the pub. **Please see the end of this issue**.

Please view it with caution as it's in HD so quite scary and hardly flattering. Oh the joy, however, to see the inside of a pub, a pulled pint (4 pints in fact) and some splendid nosh ... Steak & Guinness Pie with all the trimmings and finished off with Apple Crumble and Custard. (Takeaway, of course.)

I had to have my pudding elsewhere, however, as it said on the menu ... 'Leave room for dessert!!' 😄 Then washed down with hand-pulled real ale ... BLISS!!!! Fully legal and adhering to social distancing rules, of course.

Current Trends – Baking

Everybody's doing it. I won't link the many different articles this week (The Guardian supplement was one of many), but it really is the flavour of the month/lockdown. For obvious reasons, I suppose.

Not for me, though. The last time I tried making dough (over 20 years ago), I immediately needed the toilet. I ended up with brown fingers, coz I needed a poo!!!!! 😄

Mr T(rump)

Is it just me (and I don't wanna get too political yet), but the thing this week that fills me with dread and hilarity in equal measure, are the performances of Mr T (and, of course, I don't mean BA from the A-Team). Although with a name like TRUMP, if he WAS in the A-Team, he would have to be BO Baracus!! 😄 Anyway, how do you make jokes about a man when everything he does is more absurd than reality itself?

As I speak, I'm listening to the president on BBC News. It's another doozie of a press conference. He has just said … 'If I hadn't been elected, we would be at war with North Korea. Maybe the world would be over … hopefully with a victory' ... **Not** 😹.

Trump's End!!

There is a (better) joke in here as a heading, perhaps …

Let me know if you can think of one 😹

Perhaps the best thing to do is to lower him into some quick-drying cement. That would, however, set a really bad president!!!! 😄

Seriously though, it's a shame that Andrew Cuomo isn't running for president, as his performances have put Trumpy to shame.

I'm in love with a German … ***** … what could it be?**

Please see the following article …

https://www.theguardian.com/media/2020/apr/14/
the-sun-woman-attraction-to-chandeliers-not-a-

sexual-orientation-ipso-says

Again, how can you tell jokes (even crap ones) when reality is stranger than fiction?

Anyway, it was suggested that this could have been one of my gags, and I should come up with a punchline. So, I'll hand it over to you all and give it a go for next week. **Anybody wanna have a go? Perhaps this story could be the punchline itself.** There is a prize for the winner. Next time I see you. 👬

Darts ... 'Let's ... play ... socially ... responsible ... darts.'

Home League https://www.pdc.tv/

It started on Friday but is continuing every night. A chance to see some 'sport' and perhaps place a bet (wow!). It continues every night and is free on pdc/tv ... see above link. It's perhaps a little bit strange without the Audience Participation and the high-tech cameras ... but it's a start.

In next week's issue, I'll tell you about when I played a few legs on the oche with the lead singer of the Bangles (Suzanna Hoffs). When scoring, however, she chalks like an Egyptian!!!! 😄

Next Week's Films/TV

The wonderful Killing Eve (Series 3) starts on Sunday (As mentioned, the first episode is already on the iPlayer).

Ashes To Ashes continues on the Drama Channel, and you can get this and Life On Mars (prequel, of sorts) all on Netflix (and probably elsewhere).

Myself and the missus are currently watching both series back-to-back. Fortunately for me, I'm the one facing the TV. 😄 Seriously, probably one of my favourites on TV of all time (sic).

Midnight Run (Film 4) and the Court Jester (Talking Pictures) are both on Wed 22nd.

Word of the Day/Week ... to return next week.

Nuff for now????!!!!

Keep safe.

Stevie

135

Issue No 5

Sunday 26th April 2020

Trump Says to Drink Bleach!!!!

Headlines:

- ▶ Boris Johnson returns to face critics amid talk of the 'new normal'
- ▶ PM back in No 10 as ministers warn physical distancing is here to stay after lockdown

Hi,

Ok?

Malities, malities, malities, malities …

That's the formalities out of the way. 😂

That Was The Week That Was (TWTWTW)

Many 'stranger than fiction' issues again this week. *'Truth IS often stranger than fiction, but it is because Fiction is obliged to stick to possibilities; Truth isn't.'* (Mark Twain)

- ▶ Being a smoker could give some defence against CV-19. http://www.rfi.fr/en/science-and-technology/20200423-french-researchers-suggest-nicotine-could-protect-against-covid-19
- ▶ Last week on TV. Cooking with Cannabis (Netflix).
- ▶ Oil is cheaper than toilet paper (in fact, cheaper

than everything). This could put the skids under investments!! 😂

Toilet Rolls

Who would have thought we would be (still) talking so much about this? I just can't get to the bottom of it!! 😂

I ran out of toilet roll again this week, so I was reduced to wiping my bum with lettuce leaves. That's just the tip of the iceberg!!!! 😂

CV-19, however, has given me a certain perspective on life as I'm now content to just get hold of any shopping/toilet rolls. Even using 1-ply will do. The latter really has helped me get in touch with my inner self, though. 😂

Even Personal Ads are Changing

I saw a personal ad this week (No you didn't, Steve!!). Single man with multiple packs of toilet rolls, would like to meet a girl with hand sanitizer for some good, clean fun. 😂

In Love With A German ********** Last Week's Edition (see attached) 👬

Last week's Audience Participation 👬 section was about a German woman in love with a German Chandelier ... see https://www.theguardian.com/media/2020/apr/14/the-sun-woman-attraction-to-chandeliers-not-a-sexual-orientation-ipso-says.

Thanks for all your returns. The winning answer was ... **Her(r) High Light of the Week!** Winner Mr C. Capon(e). His reward is a (sur)prize, so you will have to wait until he gets/opens it.

A Bit of Culture ... My Poem of the Week

I'm in Love with a Brown Paper Bag by John Hegley. See the end of this issue.

There is a link with the above 'chandelier' 'story (in love with strange objects), and it IS one of my favourite poems/verses (The ONLY one, actually, as I'm not into poetry). I genuinely used to recite/sing this in the car with my daughter years ago (sic).

Mr T(rump)

A regular feature of this newsletter, I was, however, genuinely not going to put him in this week until his suggestion that an injection of bleach could help cure/prevent CV-19. Obviously, I am paraphrasing, but hardly doing him any kind of disservice ...

His aides initially tried to defend him and said he was being misquoted and taken out of context, BUT sort of blown out of the water later when Trump came out and said, he was 'just being sarcastic and goading the media'!!!

Trump down the Toilet?

Perhaps he could have just said he was trying to give a boost to the bleach industry as it was going down the toilet!! AND that he was being sarcastic because if you drink bleach, you basically dye! 😂

Acid (Bleach) Test!!

Perhaps it IS the time to start drinking bleach when an incumbent president of the US of A –

- ► Points to his head coz he can't say/remember the word 'intelligence.'
- ► Decides he is not bothering with his daily press conference, takes his 'ball home,' and won't let anyone else use it!!!!!!!!!! And, of course,
- ► Tells people to drink bleach.

Oh dear!!!!!

Businesses in Turmoil ... Hairdressers Highlighted this Week

- ► You may have seen tutorials or supplements this week on how to cut your own hair in lockdown. Learning to cut our own or live with unkempt hair is not the only reason there might be issues in hairdressing.
- ► Many are expecting cuts!!!
- ► Barber queues are not allowed!!

They will be offering 20% off ... but I'm not sure how they can be so exact. 😂

Some Other Businesses that Might Struggle...

- ► Template factory workers – will have their work cut out for them.

- ► Sculpture studios – might go bust.
- ► Trampolines – will have their ups and downs.
- ► Clown shoe manufacturers staying in business – no small feat.
- ► Lumberjacks – might not be able to hack it and/or get the axe.
- ► Tailors – might not be suited after lockdown for such a so-so job.

And you know what could happen to postmen? 😂

Next Week … Dentists in decay and their flossophy!!!!!!!!!!

👥 **Any other suggestions? A prize for the best.**

Back to Reality …

Hairdressers, though, are starting to reopen in the State of Georgia (and elsewhere in the USA) from today. BNAG … It's Bang out of order!! 😂

Speaking of bangs!! Gun sales are soaring in the US as governors are accused of using CV as a way of keeping gun shops closed to force them out of business. You couldn't make it up!!!

Do Gun Shops get Held Up? A Genuine Question

I've never thought of this before, but has there ever been a hold-up in a gun store? There must have been!! I've never even seen a joke sketch based on this idea, but there must be some material here. One for later issues, perhaps??!!

141

🏠 Has anyone ever seen anything on this?

Next Week

TV/Films

- ▶ Once upon a Time In Hollywood - Friday 1st, Sky
- ▶ Notorious ... Talking Pictures Tuesday 28th 7 pm.
- ▶ The Full Monty ... BBC1 Friday 1st 10.45 pm.

Next Week's Issue:

- ▶ Schooling the Kids from Home ... Maths and English at least
- ▶ Dentists
- ▶ Word of the Week
- ▶ Crap Joke Bingo and much more.
- ▶ And no more Mr T(rump) ... I'll try!!!

Cast, cast, cast, cast ... That's the forecast, anyway. See what I did there (again)???!!!!!

Stay safe

Byeeeeeeeeeeeeeeeee

Stevie

PS ... Good news? I've finally found a way of cutting down the length of this weekly newsletter ... I'll do it twice a week!!!!!!! 😅

***He's in Love With a Brown Paper Bag* by John Hegley**
...

his mother she was disappointed
it's not exactly what she had in mind
but eventually she came to except it
how could a mother reject it
he's in love and love isn't easy to find
people stop and people stare
people say they're a crazy pair
but there's many a crazy scene
between a husband and a wife

he found it by a market stall
it's a bit screwed up but aren't we all
an empty bag is an empty life
and he doesn't mind if you caress
his little scrap of happiness
he's in love but he doesn't want to possess

and one day he came up to me
he held the bag so tenderly
and he held it out to me
and I said thanks a lot
but I don't think i could cope
I've already got a steady relationship
with a light blue envelope
it was nice of you to offer though

Issue No 6

Sunday 3rd May 2020

My Daughter's 25th Birthday Special Edition!!!

Headline:

- ▶ Revealed: Year Six primary school pupils may return on 1st June
- ▶ Coronavirus UK: health passports 'possible in months'

Hi,

By the way, Lionel Ritchie has been in touch and says 'Hello' **(see also at (⌣|⌣) X1)**. Next week - Adele says Hello as well but crosses the road first! **(See (⌣|⌣) X2 if you need to.)**

Something is missing!!!

We are now into Week 6 of the lockdown/newsletter (wow!!!), and I have realised there was something missing … and that something is … 'laughter.' Not yours, of course, as when did you ever laugh at anything I said? More importantly, when did I care?! No, the laughter is all mine!!!!

Anyway, so I have introduced a new high-tech function. Wherever you see 😊, you will then be prompted (as always, just like in t'pub) when a so-called joke has actually happened. It'll be like old times … pre-

145

lockdown.

In this Week's Issue

There is a section on what is coming up in this week's issue!!!!!!!!!

- ► 1. Feedback ... Your Responses.
- ► 1a. Businesses in Trouble x2
- ► 2. English Corner (Where's your Grammar?)
- ► 3. (New) Villains of the Peace. A Couple of Complete and Utter B's
- ► 4. Get Well Soon, Me/Stevie P!!
- ► 5. Quiz ... AP 👫
- ► 6. The Serious Bit ... Some Sad News.

Unlike my Chicken Pellet Business, I've had some FEEDBACK. 😂

Yes, you have been in touch in your thousands!!!

Firstly, some kind words!!

- ► 'I was looking at the scroll bar on the right of the screen thinking this must be a really long poem at the bottom, but nope, the crap jokes keep going on and on and on.' Colin C - an avid reader!!

For those now checking the scroll bar ... don't worry; it's only this long because of the quiz at (⌣|⌣) **X3**. It's 15 pages long??!!

Businesses in Trouble x2

Also, I had some responses to last week's AP regarding Businesses in Trouble x1. See below:

▶ Butchers – facing the chop.
▶ Timpson, and many other locksmiths, are insisting they should reopen as they are 'key' workers.
▶ Historians – have no future.
▶ Screwfix direct – diversifying as a dating agency

Some Good News...

One colleague genuinely replied and said he can't do his day job now, so ... 'I've started a boat building business based in my loft. Sales have gone through the roof.'

I also received this from a water pressure company this week ... everyone's at it with these gags, and some are serious.

Water Jetting Contractor still
Maintains the Pressure

Good Afternoon,

Following the recent Government updates regarding the ongoing COVID-19 situation we would like to assure our customers that we are continuing to work during these testing times.

All our work is undertaken following the strict guidelines to ensure all operatives remain as safe as possible during works.

Our normal suite of water jetting services are still available, while all requirements will be reviewed on an individual basis. This ensures all guidelines not only within the Water Jetting Association but also those specified by the Government are followed.

We hope you stay safe during these testing times and look forward to working with you in the future under more normal circumstances.

Best regards,

Jobs in Jeopardy

Not to worry, the headline in the paper this morning said … 'Thousands of Jobs in Jeopardy.' So, all those being laid off, just go there!!! 😂

English Corner … Where's Your Grammar?
(see (‿|‿) X4)

Word of the Week - see (‿|‿) X7

Vanilla **…**

It's interesting to see the second definition of this. Often heard it used and probably even used it myself. But is this the context (we) meant/intended?

It's something I often consider (sad, I know), but there are many words used in everyday phrases that are very seldom used in everyday use and, when challenged, do we really know the meaning? A couple I often highlight are –

▶ Dulcet Tones
▶ Ulterior Motive

AP ... 👥 Without looking them up, do you know what 'tones' and 'motive'... only kidding ... 'dulcet' and 'ulterior' actually mean? Are you just guessing from the phrase? You might be surprised ... or is it just me being thick? Let me know what you think and if there are any others.

I'll tell you next week if you can't be bothered checking before.

Next Week

Maths (Backed into a) Corner ... **'Wanna Fight = 7' ??** ... An easy one to start with as a taster!!!! **(see (‿|‿) X5)** if you can't work it out.

(New) Villains of the Peace!!!

No Mr T, 'That Guy from the USA,' this week (I'm sure he'll be back).

True to my word, I will not mention Mr T (Oops!) as he doesn't seem to have 'outdone himself' this week yet!!! Unlike Mr Whippy, who was found dead today on the floor of his ice-cream van! His head was covered with sprinkles & chocolate sauce. Police believe he may have 'topped' himself. 😬

This week, my frustration turns towards others.

There are a few Bs around!!

Branson

If you believe there is a bearded old man in the sky looking out for us, you will have had your hopes dashed this week!!! Allegedly, Branson has started his own charity (by himself/for himself) by walking around his private island 100 times to save his net worth as it plummets towards £4 billion. Why don't you do what everyone else does in times of trouble and 'liquidate some assets??!!!' Or lose some wealth.

They Give Kids a Bad Name ... The Beckhams 💩

The Beckhams seem happy to do 'charity' when it promotes their image and, therefore, ultimately, their fortune. They are not as keen, however, when it means paying for no return on their fortune or, perhaps, even just paying their staff wages (instead of furloughing 'em and asking the taxpayer to 'cough up').

A late volte-face on their decision does nothing to mitigate the initial choice. They know public criticism will hit their brand. So, it just compounds the hypocrisy!!!

And there are many more (and more will surface). Question ... **What happened to 'Means Testing' and Naming and Shaming, Shakers and shirkers, etc.!! Why does it not apply equally here!!??**

Is Kim Jong-Un Dead, or is Kim Jong-Un.... the Undead?! 😅

Apparently, his Korea isn't over and he hasn't emigrated to South Korea to see his Seoul mate!! 😅

As a new imminent threat smoulders between North and South Korea, shots are fired on the border (there are very few headlines about this, given everything else going on). Reports of Kim's death appear to have been 'Grossly Exaggerated.' He has apparently appeared in public for the first time in 3 weeks.

▶ NB. The only way, perhaps, to tell if KJU has 'snuffed it,' and a lesson for all, is to monitor breathing constantly. Especially given that in a recent CV-19 survey, the LATEST stats confirm that 100% of deaths are due to lack of breath!!! 😅

Get Well Soon Me/Stevie P.

A Remarkable Recovery. It was so weird for me watching the news!!! (‿|‿) X6)

https://www.bbc.co.uk/news/uk-england-dorset-52501985

Quiz … see (‿|‿) X3 📸

Included by popular demand. Given that my mates don't turn up (even virtually) for mine, I've had to call on a statistician to make up the numbers. 😅

Thanks to Ben R for the questions.

Answers next week, or earlier if you ask nicely!!!!!!!!!!
And you'll be glad to hear lots of quiz jokes?!

Let me know how many you score (honestly) and a prize for the winner. It's not open to those who have seen it before. Although many might still get most wrong, given how 'thick' you are!!

NB. Please pass on or use this/anything else in this email to stave off the boredom. You do know my views on plagiarism, DON'T YOU?! If not, see next week's issue.

The Serious Bit (Seriously)

Many more have died this week, but a special mention for Jon Merrills (a colleague) and Trevor Cherry (another Leeds Legend), who have also sadly passed away this week. RIP both/all.

Next week's Cast Cast Cast Cast (forecast) will be back next week as this week's edition is already too long. 'No, it's not, Steve!!!!???'

That's all, folks. (Thank God, Steve!!)

Regards,

Keep safe,

Steve

(◡|◡) **X1** or 'Lionel Richtea!!! Is it tea you're looking for?' as it says on the mug at work.

(◡|◡) **X2** Adele says, 'Hello from the other side.'

(‿|‿) **X3 Quiz Questions** 👥 If you can be bothered!

Politics

1. How many heads are carved into Mount Rushmore?
2. What year was John Major made leader of the Conservative Party?
3. In what city was Boris Johnson born?
4. And in what year?
5. Who is the current Shadow Chancellor of the Exchequer?
6. What is the animal symbol for the American Republican Party?
7. Donald Trump won the Republic Primary in 2016; who came 3rd?
8. Who was the last UK-serving politician to be arrested? Clue, it was in 2019.
9. Bonus point if you can name the constituency.
10. Who were the six founding members of the EU (1/2 a point for each)

Possible points = 12

Music

1. 'Divinely Uninspired to a Hellish Extent' is the debut album of which Scottish singer-songwriter?
2. Which artist is currently the most all-time listened to on Spotify?
3. Which US rapper had 1998 hits with 'Gettin' Jiggy Wit It,' 'Just The Two Of Us' and 'Miami'?
4. Which group released 'We Built This City' in

1985?

5.   Who sang 'My Green Tambourine' in 1967?

6.   What award did masked metal band, Slipknot, win in 2006?

7.   'Bridge Over Troubled Water' was the title of the final album from which musical duo?

8.   In which year did Rush release their debut album, Bob Dylan toured for the first time since 1966 and Mick Taylor left the Rolling Stones?

9.   What does the MOBOs stand for?

10. Artist Dave received criticism for his recent performance at the Brits, but why?

Possible Points = 10

Sport

1.   What diameter is the circle from which you throw a discus?

2.   In which sport might you come across an albatross?

3.   What type of bowler might use a chinaman?

4.   How much were England Rugby fined for crossing the halfway line during the New Zealand haka at the 2020 World Cup?

5.   How many points are Leeds United currently on?

6.   If you had £14 in your Sky Bet bank account and bet it all on a horse to win at 7/2, what would it return?

7.   Name the Rugby Union trophy for which England and Scotland compete.

8. In Olympic Weight Lifting, what are the two methods of lifting? (Both answered are needed for a point)

9. Who, in football, is the highest scoring defender of all time?

10. Six teams have won the Premier League; one player has played for four of them but never won the league. Who is it? As a clue, he finished his career at Leeds United. (2 points on offer)

Possible Points = 11

The answers will be in the next issue.

(‿|‿) **X4** 'Upstairs, Shaaaggg-, erm, I mean … with Grandpa!!'

(‿|‿) **X5** One off 8=7!

(‿|‿) **X6** Not really me, of course.

(‿|‿) **X7** Vanilla

vanilla

adjective | vuh-NILL-uh

Definition

1 **:** flavored with the extract of the vanilla bean

2 **:** lacking distinction **:** plain, ordinary, conventional

Did You Know?

How did vanilla get such a bad rap? The flavor with that name certainly has enough fans, with the bean of the *Vanilla* genus of orchids finding its way into products ranging from ice cream to coffee to perfumes to air fresheners. Vanilla's unfortunate reputation arose due to its being regarded as the "basic" flavor among ice-cream selections, particularly as more complex flavors emerged on the market. (Its somewhat beigey color probably didn't help.) From there, people began using the adjective to describe anything plain, ordinary, or conventional.

Examples of VANILLA

"Training for sales, marketing and installation staff takes place in a series of small conference rooms on one side of the floor.... They're rather *vanilla*, but the company plans to enliven them by hiring graffiti artists to paint colorful murals on the parapet wall outside the windows." — Sandy Smith, *Philadelphia Magazine*, 14 Feb. 2019

"Joanna is frustrated that she's forbidden from sending more personal replies and breaks the rules at a certain point, with unexpected consequences. But apart from this tiny transgression, she's too *vanilla* to be a very compelling character." — Peter DeBruge, *Variety*, 20 Feb. 2020

Issue No 7
Sunday 10th May 2020

Banksy's Game Changer for NHS

Headlines:

▶ Boris Johnson's lockdown release is condemned as divisive, confusing and vague

▶ Sturgeon reveals irritation over Whitehall lockdown messaging

Hi,

Okay? You can tell me (**see** (‿|‿) **X1** Croc Dundee).

Apologies if you received the newsletter more than once last week. It was so good; I sent it three times!!!! Seriously, there was a technical glitch and some had difficulty receiving my 'Comedy Cone Chortle' (CCC).

I've attached it again, to be used when you see 😂. Alternatively, use it if just want to hear my lovely laugh!! As you know, I am in court next week for being egotistical. But I am appealing!! 😂

Coming up in this Issue –

▶ CV19 Lingo

▶ Banksy's Game Changer

▶ Where's Your Grammar?/Word of the Week (WOTW) - Plagiarism (finally!!!)

▶ Quiz - Answers from Issue 6 and New Qs. Well

done, Mr Magoo, erm, sorry, Magog!
- ▶ Stevie's Faaaaaact of the Weeeeeek!
- ▶ Potential Areas of Optimism... Wildlife and Astronomy
- ▶ Maths (Backed into a) Corner. Home Schooling for Kids/Adults?
- ▶ Next Week - Footy Returns? TV and Films.
- ▶ (‿|‿)(‿|‿)(‿|‿)

CV-19 Lingo (see (‿|‿) X3)

Isn't it strange how we (or was it just me!) used to cough to hide a fart, and now we fart to hide a cough?! They've not invented a word for that yet!

There's some good lingo here as we remain in lockdown and cases continue to rise in the UK. Only the fall in hospital admissions seems to be a slightly optimistic figure. That's only because the Govt has decided that not everyone injured in a peek-a-boo accident needs to go to the ICU!!! 😆

Banksy's Game Changer

We are all looking for a game changer, though ... and I don't mean eating pheasant instead of quail!! 😆 But we did have one of sorts this week - see the below link (courtesy of Banksy).

https://www.theguardian.com/artanddesign/2020/may/06/banksy-artwork-superhero-nurse-nhs-coronavirus-covid-19-southampton-general-hospital

A new work of art and dedicated to the NHS. It will ultimately be sold to raise funds. I love it. I think I'll get myself a copy.

Where's Your Grammar? - Word of the Week (WOTW)

Speaking of Copying. Following weeks of mentioning that 'You know my views on plagiarism,' this week, I was actually prompted (Surely not, Steve) to explain what 'I was on about.' So, I made it WOTW. See the below link.

Plagiarism https://en.wikipedia.org/wiki/Plagiarism

'Actually, I invented the word only a few days ago.' Someone else's words, not mine. 😊

But I DO believe that a day will come when plagiarism won't exist ...

> ... You may say I'm a dreamer
> But I'm not the only one!!

Anyway, anyone who says I nick their material can kiss my black ass. 😄

NB ... If You Steal from One, It's Plagiarism; If You Steal from Many, It's Research!!!

Maths (Backed into a) Corner

Wanna Fight = 7 **(see (⌣|⌣) X2)**

Homeschooling. Not telling you how to suck eggs, but ...

Did you know that multiplying by 11 is easy? All you do is add up the digits of the 'other' number and place it in between.

So, 11x12=1(3)2, 11x21=2(3)1, etc. There are some limitations but it's quite 'handy' (fingery), perhaps?

I've known this for many years but probably didn't know it when I needed it most (at school)!!!!!!!!!!!!!!! **Was this new to you? For kids or adults?**

Next week

Why was 6 afraid of 7? **Again, for kids and adults, perhaps?**

Quiz (keeping with the theme and absolutely no help from Mr B Robinson!!). Please have a go at the questions yourself and (honestly) tell me how many you get. Then, blatantly use them as often as you like and claim credit for them (keeping with today's theme of plagiarism)!!!

Answers to last week and a Music Song Title Quiz (see end of issue).

Quiz Questions Answers

Politics

1. How many heads are carved into Mount Rushmore? – 4

2. What year was John Major made leader of the Conservative Party? – 1990

3. In what city was Boris Johnson born? – New

York

4.   And in what year? – 1964

5.   Who is the current Shadow Chancellor of the Exchequer? – Anneliese Dodd

6.   What is the animal symbol for the American Republican Party? – Elephant

7.   Donald Trump won the Republic Primary in 2016; who came 3rd? – Marco Rubio

8.   Who was the last UK-serving politician to be arrested? Clue, it was in 2019 – Jared O'Mara.

9.   Bonus point if you can name the constituency – Sheffield Hallam

10. Who were the six founding members of the EU? (1/2 a point for each)

Belgium, France, West German, Italy, Luxembourg, Netherlands

Possible points = 12

Music

1.   'Divinely Uninspired to a Hellish Extent' is the debut album of which Scottish singer-songwriter? – Lewis Capaldi

2.   Which artist is currently the most all time listened to on Spotify – Ed Sheeran

3.   Which US rapper had 1998 hits with 'Gettin' Jiggy Wit It', 'Just The Two Of Us' and 'Miami'? – Will Smith

4.   Which group released 'We Built This City' in 1985? – Starship

5. Who sang 'My Green Tambourine' in 1967? – The Lemon Pipers

6. What award did masked metal band, Slipknot, win in 2006? – Grammy

7. 'Bridge Over Troubled Water' was the title of the final album from which musical duo? – Simon & Garfunkel

8. In which year did Rush release their debut album, Bob Dylan toured for the first time since 1966 and Mick Taylor left the Rolling Stones? – 1974

9. What does the MOBOs stand for? – Music of Black Origin

10. Artist Dave received criticism for his recent performance at the Brits, but why? – Accusing the prime minister of racism

Possible Points = 10

Sport

1. What diameter is the circle from which you throw a discus? – 2.5m

2. In which sport might you come across an albatross? – Golf

3. What type of bowler might use a chinaman? – A legspin bowler

4. How much were England Rugby fined for crossing the half way line during the New Zealand haka at the 2020 World Cup? – £2,000

5. How many points are Leeds United currently

on? – 71

6.   If you had £14 in your Sky Bet bank account and bet it all on a horse to win at 7/2, what would it return? – 49 plus stake

7.   Name the Rugby Union trophy for which England and Scotland compete – Calcutta Cup

8.   In Olympic Weight Lifting, what are the two methods of lifting? – Clean & Jerk, The Snatch (Both answers are needed for a point)

9.   Who, in football, is the highest scoring defender of all time? – Ronald Koeman

10. Six teams have won the Premier League; one player has played for four of them but never won the league. Who is it? As a clue, he finished his career at Leeds United – Paul Dickov (2 points on offer)

Possible Points = 11

Well done Mr N Magog with the highest score of the week … a drink of your choice awaits you (after lockdown).

NB. Definitions for the words Dulcet and Ulterior are (from last issue) –

dulcet

/ˈdʌlsɪt/

adjective

1. (especially of sound) sweet and soothing (often used ironically).

"record the **dulcet tones** of your family and friends»

ulterior

/ʌlˈtɪərɪə/

adjective

1.   existing beyond what is obvious or admitted; intentionally hidden.

"could there be an **ulterior motive** behind his request?»

🎵 Stevie's Faaaaact of the Weeeeeek!! 🎵
(Again, all my own work and nothing to do with Kev)

With an egg white, a syringe and a pump, you can mend busted footballs (sic).

Potential Areas of Optimism (in the Lockdown Gloom). Wildlife and Astronomy

I'll try to mention both items, but I might run out of time and space for the second. 😂

FYI - In 1905, Einstein developed a theory about space … and it was about time too!! 😂

Wildlife

This week: The Birds

We seem to be seeing some amazing sights as the wildlife enjoys new freedom. This is especially true with birds.

Havoc at the Bird Feeder (Sounds like a pop group?!)

A colleague told me (sic) this week that there is a daily brawl with the birds in his garden over birdseed, and the feeder often gets knocked to the ground.

That reminds me, I must finish my bird table that I started in lockdown. The wife's not going to be happy when she finds out she's slipped to 6th place, though! 😆

Pigeons

In addition, it has been reported in town centres that pigeons (bereft of food) are swooping down on those that are there, like a scene from Hitchcock's 'The Birds.' Conversely, many are concerned over their welfare and keen for them to be fed. What a reversal, from us just calling them vermin and wanting them exterminated!!!

Solution: To find food, they just need to drive off in their new cars. Let's face it; they have been putting down deposits on them for years. 😆

Final Quiz Question. What is the most common owl in the world? (⌣|⌣) **X4**

Next Week

Special Issue - Football is Back ... whether you like it or not!!!

Bundesliga Returns ... or does it? See https://www.

theguardian.com/football/2020/may/09/bundesliga-restart-blow-dynamo-dresden-team-quarantined-covid-19?CMP=Share_AndroidApp_WhatsApp.

Films/TV

Moonlight. Wed 9 pm Film 4

Robocop 9 pm Thursday

See ya soon …

Stay safe.

Stevie

Not as many bums this week!!!!!

(⌣|⌣) **X1** 'If you got a problem, you can tell me and I tell everyone. Brings it out in the open, no more problems'!!!! Once again, nicked (and slightly altered) from Croc Dundee the movie!

(⌣|⌣) **X2** – One off 8 = 7! Just in case you missed last week

(⌣|⌣) **X3** – Lockdown Lingo (below)

(⌣|⌣) **X4** – The most common owl in the world is: the Teat. In most/all kitchens in the land. 😸

Lockdown Lingo - are you fully conversant with the new terminology?

Coronacoaster

The ups and downs of your mood during the pandemic. You're loving lockdown one minute but suddenly weepy with anxiety the next. It truly is "an emotional coronacoaster."

Quarantinis

Experimental cocktails mixed from whatever random ingredients you have left in the house. The boozy equivalent of a store cupboard supper. Southern Comfort and Ribena quarantini with a glacé cherry garnish, anyone? These are sipped at "locktail hour," i.e. wine o'clock during the lockdown, which seems to be creeping earlier with each passing week.

Le Creuset Wrist

167

It's the new "avocado hand" - an aching arm after taking one's best saucepan outside to bang during the weekly 'Clap For Carers.' It might be heavy, but you're keen to impress the neighbours with your high-quality kitchenware.

Coronials

As opposed to millennials, this refers to the future generation of babies conceived during coronavirus quarantine. They might also become known as "Generation C" or, more spookily, "Children of the Quarn."

Furlough Merlot

Wine consumed in an attempt to relieve the frustration of not working. Also known as "bored-eaux" or "cabernet tedium."

Coronadose

An overdose of bad news from consuming too much media during a time of crisis. It can result in a panicdemic.

The Elephant in the Zoom

The glaring issue during a videoconferencing call that nobody feels able to mention. E.g. one participant has dramatically put on weight, suddenly sprouted terrible facial hair or has a worryingly messy house visible in the background.

Quentin Quarantino

An attention-seeker using their time in lockdown to make amateur films which they're convinced are funnier and cleverer than they actually are.

Covidiot or *Wuhan-ker*

One who ignores public health advice or behaves with reckless disregard for the safety of others can be said to display "covidiocy" or be "covidiotic". Also called a "lockclown" or even a "Wuhan-ker."

Goutbreak

The sudden fear that you've consumed so much wine, cheese, homemade cake and Easter chocolate in lockdown that your ankles are swelling up like a medieval king's.

Antisocial distancing

Using health precautions as an excuse for snubbing neighbours and generally ignoring people you find irritating.

Coughin' dodger

Someone so alarmed by an innocuous splutter or throat-clear that they back away in terror.

Mask-ara

Extra make-up applied to "make one's eyes pop" before venturing out in public wearing a face mask.

Covid-10

The 10 kgs in weight that we're all gaining from

comfort-eating and comfort-drinking. Also known as "fattening the curve."

Music Song Title Quiz

Example: ***"Today is gonna be the day that they're gonna throw it back to you."*** *Song title starts with W.*

Answer – Wonderwall by Oasis

1. "She played the fiddle in an Irish band but she fell in love with an English man." – G.G.

2. "They're out to get you, better leave while you can, don't wanna be a boy, you wanna be a man." – B.I.

3. "And the Christmas bells that ring there are the clanging chimes of doom." – D.T.K.I.C

4. "Remember to let her into your heart, then you can start to make it better." – H.J.

5. "There's a fire starting in my heart, reaching a fever pitch and it's bringing me out the dark." – R.I.T.D

6. "Life is a mystery, everyone must stand alone." – L.A.P

7. "See the stone set in your eyes." – W.O.W.Y.

8. "She's got a smile that it seems to me reminds me of childhood memories." – S.C.O.M

9. "There must be some kind of way out of here, said the joker to the thief." – A.A.T.W.

10. "Oh life, it's bigger, it's bigger than you." – L.M.R.

The answers will be in the next issue.

Issue No 8

Sunday 17th May 2020

Stargazing Takes Off

Headlines:

- ▶ UK plans £38m centre to start production of coronavirus vaccine
- ▶ Chelsea flower show opens online amid lockdown gardening boom

Hi,

Have I done my déjà-vu joke yet?!!!

Comic Cone Chortle (CCC) once again attached for whenever you see 😂 Or whenever you like, really (if you care)!!!! I genuinely chuckle at the chuckle every time I play it!!!

In this Issue –

- ▶ Health & Safety Moment
- ▶ There's no Future in Nostalgia - it just isn't what it used to be!!! But a little Stevie goes a long way!!!
- ▶ Stargazing. I'm over the Moon, Brian. (‿|‿) X1
- ▶ Fact of the Week (FOTW)
- ▶ Puzzle(s) of the Week and Last Week's Answers
- ▶ Maths (Backed into a Corner). Home-Schooling Tips for the Young 'Uns (and Mr Magoog!)?

- ▶ Are You a Background Bookcase Watcher? The Beautiful Poetry of Donald Trump - I Kid You not!!
- ▶ Quiz … too many puzzles/AP, so will return next week
- ▶ (⌣|⌣)(⌣|⌣)(⌣|⌣)

Health & Safety Moment

In good ol' Highways England (HE) tradition, I'm going to start with a Health and Safety Moment (as most know, a must for all HE Communications/Meetings).

Under the present circumstances, people must not cough near you, they must cough far away …

If you hear or see someone coughing near you,

Tell them to … Far Cough. 😄

There's no Future in Nostalgia … It's just not what it used to be 😄

A bit late this week getting started as my brother found an old picture (sic) on a 'I went to … School' website. Can you work out which one is me!!!?

In the second photo, spot the famous footballer – Clue: not me.

I remember this end of year photo below so well at the time because of how embarrassed I looked at being so close to someone of the opposite sex.

Obviously, I was not always one for the ladies!!! Unless, of course, when the gents are out of order!! (‿|‿) X2 😂

Given it's on the 'net,' I thought I'd share little Stevie with you above!!!!

Given we are well into lockdown, and the current situation is:

My best attempt ever of growing a beard (with little success) picture next week?!

I need a haircut

I only use two sets of clothes

I'm eating like a horse (‿|‿) X3

I've only had a shower once since lockdown began. At least this has helped with social distancing!!!

I've now grown up (????)….

So, the similarities from these photos have faded long ago!!!!!!I

Stargazing ... Was Space Cool Before It Mattered? 😂

See this quick guide https://skyandtelescope.org/astronomy-resources/stargazing-basics/how-to-start-right-in-astronomy/

I'm trying to planet better this time and I 'Apollogise' for not having the time or space (you did that one before, Steve) last week. Sa turn that frown upside down and be over the moon at the Beginner's Guide to Astronomy. I can't even bring myself to put the CCC at the end of these!!!

People do, however, seem very keen about it now and I'm not entirely sure why. Boredom, less pollution helps visibility ... or is it just because people are off work and can stay up later? **Any thoughts?**

♫ **Stevie's Faaaaact of the Weeeeeek!!** ♫

Sean Connery was banned by the car company of doing Citroen ads because of his accent/pronunciation (work it out!!!). NB. There is absolutely no link/segue with anything before or after in this email other than I remembered it when I added the Bookshelf 'joke' below.

♫ Stevie's Puzzzzzzzle ... (forget that) ...

Puzzle(s) of the Week (POTW)

Eleven plus two = twelve plus one. There are two other ways that this sentence is true other than the obvious. The clue to one is how it has been presented. The second is bizarre and I'm not sure I understand it yet ... and I know the answer!!!!

My brother has 5 children (no he doesn't, Steve) and half of them are boys, how come?

Answers on a postcard, erm, I mean, by reply to this email, please. 📇

Maths (Backed into a) Corner – 'Wanna Fight = 7' (see previous if needed)

Last Week's Answers

- 11x table. The majority had never heard of this little trick.

This week - 9x table (one for the younger audience, perhaps, and Mr Magoog). See (‿|‿) **X4** (Courtesy of The Pocster).

- Answer to last week's maths puzzle … six is afraid of 7 because 7 8 (ate) 9 and you're supposed to eat three squared (3*3=9) meals per day!!!

Fibonacci Sequence …

I thought my Fibonacci Sequence joke would be perfect at this point, but it probably won't be any better than my last two jokes put together!!! 😂

Have I done my déjà-vu joke yet?! 😂

Bookcase Watching

… the latest phenomenon

On TV, Teams or Skype, everyone is making a lot of assumptions (don't forget this is naughty!!) of other people based on their background/bookcases.

Do you have a copy in your background of Mein Holiday Kampf (Hitler's trip to Butlins!), Flower Arranging Diaries of Atilla the Hun or The Beautiful Poems of Donald Trump (only one of these is a genuine book – see below). Or are they just a mess? Or is there just a hook/shadow of where an erstwhile portrait of Dorian Gray has been recently relocated to the attic? The 'removal' shadow is even worse in the 'turning up nose' stakes than any of the above.

Anyway, to give a decent impression, I loaded my bookshelf with all my best books. It didn't work, however, as they all fell off and hit me on the head in the middle of a works Team call. BUT 'I only have my shelf to blame, though.' 😄 Best to be said in a Sean Connery-style voice.

Some of my books I show off to the world are:

- ▶ Three identical books on Memory. Work it out!!
- ▶ 'How to solve 50% of your problems.' I bought two.
- ▶ A novel titled, 'A Long Walk' by Miss D Bus.
- ▶ 'Advantageous' by Benny Fishal.
- ▶ 'Best Breakfasts' by Chris P. Bacon.
- ▶ 'Living Without Art and Culture' … by Phyllis Stein. 😄

More next week???? **Please provide yours and there's a prize for the best.** 👥

And of course, Mr Trump's book, as mentioned above

(it's genuine– see below).

https://www.amazon.co.uk/Beautiful-Poetry-Donald-Trump/dp/1786894726/ref=pd_sbs_14_4/260-4837980-1149634?_encoding=UTF8&pd_rd_i=1786894726&pd_rd_r=26f77302-f

Last Week's Music Song Title Quiz Answers

1. "She played the fiddle in an Irish band but she fell in love with an English man." Galway Girl – Ed Sheeran.

2. "They're out to get you, better leave while you can, don't wanna be a boy, you wanna be a man." Beat It – Fall Out Boy

3. "And the Christmas bells that ring there are the clanging chimes of doom." Do They Know It's Christmas? – Band Aid

4. "Remember to let her into your heart, then you can start to make it better." Hey Jude – The Beatles

5. "There's a fire starting in my heart, reaching a fever pitch and it's bringing me out the dark." Rolling in the Deep - Adele

6. "Life is a mystery, everyone must stand alone." Like a Prayer - Madonna

7. "See the stone set in your eyes." With or Without You – U2

8. "She's got a smile that it seems to me reminds me of childhood memories." Sweet Child O' Mine – Guns N' Roses

9. "There must be some kind of way out of here, said the joker to the thief." All Along the Watchtower – Jimi Hendrix

10. "Oh life, it's bigger, it's bigger than you." Losing My Religion – REM

Next Week

Return of Where's your Grammar and Word of the Week … I bet you can't wait!!!!???

English football. It's already back!!! Since the easing of restrictions, allowing families to play football together, matches between Norwich and Ipswich have already recommenced. 😄 Did you also know, the Marriage Guidance Counselling Service in Norwich is called 'Related'. … Sorry DC!! 😄

Did I already do my déjà-vu joke? Do it next week?!

TV/Films

Pulp Fiction … Sony Movies, Monday at 9 pm

Tropic Thunder … BBC1, Friday at 11.15 pm

Stay safe,

Stevie

Only four bums this week

(⌣|⌣) **X1** For footy fans, a sort of predecessor to 'Unbelievable Jeff.'

(⌣|⌣) **X2** Walked into the toilets the other day (no you didn't, Steve, as the building has been shut for months!!) and a cubicle door whacked me in the face. It was 'Out of Order'!!

(⌣|⌣) **X3** Have you ever been halfway through eating a horse before realising you weren't as hungry as you first thought? I actually part-own a horse (sic) - see below.

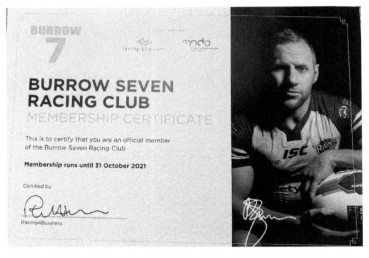

At going to 'print,' please also see the TV programme *Living with MD* on the BBC. Rob, along with Kevin Sinfield (see elsewhere), is a true legend.

(‿|‿) **X4** Help with 9 times table (see below)

Trick for the 9 Times Table ... Courtesy of Mr Poc

Put all 10 fingers up in front of you, palms facing you.

Lower your left thumb and you will see 9 handsome digits = 1x9 is 9

Now you've mastered 1x9, let's try the 2x9.

Again, put all 10 fingers up in front of you, palms facing you.

Lower the 2nd digit along. If you're doing this correctly, it should be the fore finger of your left hand. You will have 1 digit a gap and then 8 digits. 2x9 =18.

You'll find this works all the way along, so you can do your 9 times table all the way up to 9x10.

Now, where's my f*@!?#g prize?

Issue No 9

Special BH Bumper Edition for No Reason Whatsoever

Headlines:

▶ Johnson's defence of Cummings sparks anger from allies and opponents alike

Hi,

By request, I am sending this issue a little earlier in the day before beddy-byes. Luckily for all, a real bumper edition, given as I've had an extra day off????!!!!!

In this Issue –

▶ Happy Birthday, Steve!!!

▶ Back to School … Where do Teachers Stand, and are Schools Out … or in?

▶ Stevie's Song Challenge (SSC)

▶ Dominic Cummings (non-political?!)

▶ Hand Sanitiser … HOW MUCH????!!!

▶ Last Week's Puzzles and Fact of the Week (FotW)

▶ Next Week … TV, etc

▶ (⌣|⌣)(⌣|⌣)(⌣|⌣)

That's enough for now, Steve!!!!

First to NB. To all stargazers ... A Space Station went over, and it was very clear last night). On Wednesday night, you can see a manned rocket en route to the SS. I mention this now (instead of later) just in case don't make it to the end of the email!!!!!).

Happy today? Statistically speaking, did you know that 85% of dwarves aren't? Work it out!! (‿|‿) **X1.**

😸 Comedy Cone Chortle (CCC) is once again attached for your convenience!!!!!

Happy Birthday, Steve!!!!

Speaking of Happy! It was my Happy (in lockdown?!) Birthday yesterday. Thank you for all your kind words and gifts!! I was officially ... cough, cough and a 1/6th-years-old!!! My full Birthday was on Lockdown Day in March, so I missed my usual (month of) celebrations. To be fair, I have Happy Birthday clapped myself many times since, so I must now be 240 (‿|‿) **X2.** 😸

Let's Get Started ...

How shall we start this week?

If it was a Pudding Race ... Sago!!

If it was a Teddy Bear Race ... Ready, Teddy, Go!! (‿|‿) **X3.** 😸

Back to School?!

(You Can Lead a Horse to Water, but A (School) Pencil Must Be Lead!!!) 😸

Chaos!! You can't force something like this *in these times.* Teachers, kids and parents must be persuaded. Everyone is at loggerheads, and a collaborative way needs to be found by all.

Keeping Control. Even if (or when) they do go back (and with kids even more spaced out in the classroom with social distancing), it won't just be the cross-eyed teachers who can't keep control of their pupils …

Where Do Teachers Stand?

Given the above, it will be even more important for teachers to decide where to stand in the classroom. Do they stand at the front where they can reach the blackboard but cannot see the kids? Or do they stand at the back where they can see the kids but can't reach the blackboard???? This problem STILL hasn't been solved.

Not B(U)Y… A LONG CHALK!!!!! 😂

Kids, parents and teachers are very nervous about going back on 1st June. Maths teachers are especially bovvered and have become constipated with the tension. You know the rest, surely (continued appropriately at the bottom). (‿|‿) **X4**.

I bet the kids will go back for the 'Best Lesson in School' by Jim Class. Added to my Shelf (to Blame) below – see the last issue.

School's out - or is it?

Link to song ... https://www.youtube.com/watch?v=2Oo8QzDHimQ In particular ...

> 🎵 School's out forever
> School's out for summer
> **School's out with fever**
> School's out completely!!!!! 🎵

Stevie's Song Challenge (SSC).

Need to come up with a better title?

Perhaps this could be an alternative to the Facebook Album challenge? Songs and lyrics could depict the current events or the situation.

Please discuss or let me know your suggestions. 👥

Dominic Cummins......

AA, National Breakdown and Green Flag ... Don't get me started!!!!! 😂

I don't want to get too political, but for someone supposedly so strategically savvy (easy for Chris Eubank to say?!), he does seem incredibly naïve. He knew many in the press and elsewhere were 'gunning' for him because of his arrogance and position. Yet he broke his own rules, appeared to believe they were beneath him and tried to lie his way out. We do need to find a way to move on. The recent afternoon's Press Conference may have helped (?), but it shouldn't have got to this.

Stevie's Song Challenge (SSC)

Again?

Keeping with the song theme ... *an attempt below to start/have a go at another song for SSC. Too contrived?* (‿|‿) **X7. Can you do any better?** 🦉

Dom's defence - went for a short drive and just got lost and ended up in Durham, relying on his wife to navigate as she can 'read maps backwards.' That's Spam 😏 (‿|‿) **X5.**

Anyway, like others, I'm washing my hands with it ... ♫ *Happy Birthday to me, etc!!!* ♫ 241!! BUT, if you do need a quick **eyesight test,** see the image at the end of this issue.

M&S Hand Sanitiser

Speaking of washing hands, the other day, I went to M&S to buy some conveyor belt dividers. Like many others, I always pick them up and place them at the checkout, but they never seem to make it into my trolley😏. The woman in front of me (who was also shopping for dividers!!) noticed the small hand sanitiser on sale at the checkout ... and said she would 'take a couple.' As there was no price, I enquired ... 'How much?'... and was told ... '£11.50'!!!!!!!!!!! I was amazed at the price but also that the woman didn't bat an eyelid and still bought two!!

M&S must be 'rubbing their hands together with fee'!!! ♫ Happy Birthday to me, etc, ♫ 242 (Wrong type of rubbing of hands, Steve)!!!!!

I was amazed again when I got back in the car, opened the paper I'd just bought and saw this …

https://www.theguardian.com/business/2020/ may/18/marks-spencer-in-row-over-hand-sanitiser- coronavirus M&S accused of exploiting Covid 19.

What a coincidence.

Last Week's Puzzle(s) of the Week (PotW)

1. Eleven plus two = twelve plus one. **As well as being a mathematical equation, both sides are also an anagram of each other alphabetically.** There is a third way, BUT it might blow your mind just reading it!!!!!!!!!!!!!! (‿|‿) **X6.**

2. My brother has five children (No, he doesn't, Steve), and half of them are boys … how come? **The other half are boys as well.**

I spoke to a colleague/friend on Monday who had already Googled the answer - a bit early to do so by then, surely? I won't say the 'cheats' name, but it begins with C and ends in olin Capon!! 😆

"I would prefer even to fail with honour than win by cheating." **Sophocles.**

Further Books for My Shelf *(to Blame).*

Thanks for the contributions; a pint awaits you, JO, the winner.

'Trips to the Toilet' … by Willie Makit and Betty Dont

'Dentistry' by Phil McCavity (a set up for the rest of my

dentist jokes next week, perhaps?!)

And 'Best Lesson to go Back to School for' by Jim Class (see above). 😄

🎵 Stevie's Faaaaact(s) of the Weeeeeek!! 🎵

The longest word in the English language has 189,819 letters.

Methionylthreonylthreonylglutaminylarginyl... isoleucine is the chemical name of the largest known protein Titin. Lexicographers have argued, however, that chemical compounds should not count. You may know that the lengthiest non-technical word is antidisestablishmentarianism, with a mere 28 letters.

BOTH wrong ... 'Smiles' is the longest as it has a mile between the first and last letters!!! 😄

One for the kids (and Nick). Why does your nose run and your feet smell?

Because you must be upside down!!!

And again ...

Word of the Week (WOTW) - Introvertish

Quite appropriate for the moment. Are you a little bit of one or t' other? Not much choice atm!

https://www.merriam-webster.com/words-at-play/words-for-being-alone/introvertish

Next Week
- ▶ Maths Corner and Where's Your Grammar are Back
- ▶ Quiz/Puzzles
- ▶ Cummings v Trump. Only allowed to mention one or the other every week?!

TV
- ▶ The Good the Bad and the Ugly on Paramount, Wed 9 pm.
  A classic. For what it's worth, one of my top ten.

Space Station

Manned link up Wednesday night (see above).

Byeeeeeeeeeeee,

Steve

There are more bums this week than asleep on a Central Park bench … and that was before CV-19!!!

(⌣|⌣) **X1** Six out of seven are not the dwarf 'Happy.'

Or, an alternative 'line,' seven dwarves are in the bath feeling Happy. So, Happy got out and they felt Grumpy!!!

(⌣|⌣) **X2** Assuming I have had a birthday every time I sing HB, then 9 (weeks) = 63 days x 3 times a day and plus my present age of 43!!! = 240!!!!

(⌣|⌣) **X3** The oldest and cleanest jokes I know and

therefore couldn't resist!

(‿|‿) **X4** Maths teachers with constipation can work it out with a pencil. Please don't chew the end of this pencil!!!!!!!

(‿|‿) **X5** 'Spam' is maps backwards.

(‿|‿) **X6** It gets even more mildly interesting. Eleven is derived from "ainlif," a medieval Germanic expression for "one left" as in one "left over" ten. And twelve comes from "twalif." So, by doing a literal translation of the Old English into modern English, you could re-write the phrases as "one left plus two" and "two left plus one" which, naturally, are anagrams of each other.

(‿|‿) **X7** SSC. New remix by Culture Club or perhaps Vulture Club for those who think the press have a lot to answer for? (‿|‿) **X9**

Stevie's Song Challenge (SSC)……

♫ Cumma Cumma Cumma Cumma Cumma … Dom Demon!!*****

You come and go, you come and go!!!! ♫

(‿|‿) **X8** Feedback from the silent majority. 'Well done, Steve. It cannot be said that you don't report both sides of the argument?!'

(‿|‿) **X9** link below and Dom's mask.

*****Given the attached DC mask!!! Or could use 'High Treason' or 'Owellian'?

Too contrived for SSC? For consistency at least,
see the original - https://www.youtube.com/
watch?v=JmcA9LIIXWw

Issue No 10

Sunday 31st May 2020

Dom Cummings and Goings

Headlines:

► Health officials make last-minute plea to stop lockdown easing in England

Hi all ... CCC is attached for your pleasure when you see this sign 😄 or whenever!!

In this Issue -

► Back to the Future ... or is it Forward to the Past?

► No F in Leadership!!

► Jacinda Ardern (the Exception?)

► Cummings and Goings (to Australia!!)

► Good the Bad (and Ugly) Routines ... Weight, Clothes ... the Pareto (80/20) Rule

► Stevie's Faaact (and Puzzles) of the Weeeeek!

► How do You Eat an Elephant (Recipe)

► (◡|◡)(◡|◡)(◡|◡)

You will probably be glad to hear that I was struggling to get started this weekend. I had a very bad case of writer's blo-

So, I stood in my garden early one morning, thinking about what to write, looking for inspiration (◡|◡) **X1** and also wondering where the sun had gone. Then it dawned on me. 😄 I needed to sort the garden out for some peas and quiet and to help me think. So, no time to moss around. Sorry!!! 😄

Back to the Future, or is it Forward to the Past? – Some Shops are Open!!!

So, after avoiding the mad rush, I went to the Garden Centre and would you believe (No, I wouldn't, Steve!!) I bumped into Michael J Fox, from the 'filums' - Back to the Future (BttF) Trilogy, relaxing with thyme on his hands.

I wasn't certain it was him as he had his Back to the Fuchsia. I couldn't check with anyone either as there was no SAGE (perhaps the PM wouldn't allow?!) advice as far as the cacti could see!! 😄

It got me thinking about the BttF Trilogy (and No 2 in particular). Was Biff's character an accurate projection of an imagined future or a depiction of Mr Trump (surely, I'm allowed to mention him in this context) there and then 30 years ago? You may recall that Biff lived in an extravagant building, not unlike Trump Tower.

Best Sequels of all time ...

What are the best 3 film sequels of all time? 👥 Do we include BttF2? **Let me know your top 3, and I'll issue the results next week.**

No F in Leadership!!!

To be fair, I could now go to the 'Usual Suspects' (staying with the filum theme, although not a sequel). But Donald almost had a 'normal' speech yesterday. In the interest of balance, however, *no effing leadership* could be said about many of the incumbents and opposition alike atm, both here and abroad.

Crucially, regardless of allegiance, we are all keen for the Govt **not** to fail on this one. This has made recent events even more difficult for us all.

New Zealand Prime Minister Jacinda Ardern (JA)

The one exception to this must be the fantastic JA. She did have a bit of a wobble this week, but only because a 5.6 magnitude earthquake hit New Zealand in the middle of one of her speeches. Massacre, eruption, pandemic and now an earthquake. No problem, for the unflappable JA. Please, can she lead us?

Cummings and Goings

This story won't seem to go away, but it looks like he's broken the rules again. He's now been seen in Australia!! See the link for his cardboard cutout at a Rugby League match in Oz!!

https://www.theguardian.com/sport/2020/may/29/dominic-cummings-cutout-appears-at-rugby-league-match-in-sydney-australia

The Good, the Bad and the Ugly Routine. *Have you put on weight? And did you watch the film on TV last week?*

Obviously, everyone's situation is different but a recent survey suggests over 50 percent have put on weight during lockdown – no sh**, Sherlock!!!?? And, whether you are eating too much or not, food has certainly become the centre of the universe.

As I keep putting on weight in lockdown, I am slowly working my way through wearing all my stolen t-shirts in the order of size ... and, for the moment, 'I'm still at Large!!'

I went to the doctors recently. He said, "Don't eat anything fatty." I said, "Like what, bacon and burgers?" He said, "No, just don't eat anything, fatty."

Ultimately, you can either get into a good or bad routine in lockdown. I've improved at cleaning my teeth, I suppose, and jogging very slowly around the park.

What's your story?

Routine with clothes ...

The Pareto or 80/20 rule (⌣|⌣) **X2** seems to be slightly awry atm on clothes as I am probably using 5% of my clothes 95% of the time (1 set goes into the wash as the other comes out).

As an old boss often said ... 'it takes seven days to make or break a habit,' so this could go on for years.

Finally, how do you eat an elephant? As we know, one

bite at a time. So, I thought I'd include a recipe below. (‿|‿) X4

♪ Stevie's Faaaaact *(and Puzzle) of the Weeeeeek!! ♪
(Keeping with the Clothes Theme)

Fact of the Week ...

Tiny Jeans Pocket

Ever wondered what that tiny extra pocket above the main front pockets in your jeans is for? Well, here's an interesting fact?! It's a watch pocket. Back in the 1800s, cowboys used to wear their watches on chains and kept them in their waistcoats. To keep them from getting broken, Levi's introduced this small pocket where they could store their watch. **Who knew?**

Puzzle

What's the difference between a well-dressed man on a bike and a poorly dressed man on a unicycle? (‿|‿) X3

A cowboy (with his watch in his tiny jeans' pocket) rides into town on Monday, stays three days and leaves on Saturday ... How come? (‿|‿) X3

Have you googled it yet, Colin???!!!!

Next week

Do I keep going jogging now Lockdown is 'easing'?

► What am I going to write? Impossible to

predict!! By Friday, I usually have an idea, but by Sunday, it's been blown out of the water.

TV

Groundhog Day (Sony Movies) 6.55 pm tomorrow. One of my faves, but it is a 'Marmite' film. 🎬

Keep safe.

Steve

(‿|‿) **X1** "Don't waste time waiting for inspiration. Begin, and inspiration will find you." **H. Jackson Brown Jr.**

In reality, this is what I did.

(‿|‿) **X2** The **Pareto principle** (also known as the **80/20 rule,** the law of the vital few, or the **principle** of factor sparsity) states that, for many events, roughly 80% of the effects come from 20% of the causes. **Pareto** developed both concepts in the context of the distribution of income and wealth among the population.

(‿|‿) **X3** Attire/A tyre. The cowboy's horse is called Saturday.

(‿|‿) **X4** (see below)...

Elephant Stew (or Michael, Pete, etc.)

This dish takes about 2 to 3 months to prepare.

Ingredients

1 Elephant
10 Warthog
4 Guineafowl
100 kilograms tomatoes
half ton potatoes
2 bags onions
100 kilograms salt
1 wheelbarrow onions (heaped)
10 litres vinegar
20 litres chutney

Method

Hunt the elephant, warthog and guineafowl. Hang the guineafowl to ripen. Cut the elephant into edible chunks (this will take about a month). Boil the warthog with other ingredients (except guineafowl) till nice and juicy. Now boil the elephant chunks over high flames till tender. (will take about four weeks) and add everything together. Boil for another 5 to 7 days.

This produces about 3,500 helpings.

Note: If the above isn't enough, add the guineafowl as well.

Note: Under no circumstances are elephants used for food in South Africa. All elephants are protected in their natural habitat in game parks. When the parks become overpopulated (elephants are very destructive to the flora), they are either re-located or undergo planned culling.

Also note ... this is not a real recipe. Just in case you come across an elephant for sale in Tesco!!!

Issue No 11

Lockdown Easing

Headlines:
- ▶ UK coronavirus victims have lain undetected at home for two weeks
- ▶ Ministers face backlash after claiming Britain is not racist

Hi ... CCC (Comic Cone Chortle) attached when you see 😅. I am experimenting with new formatting this week. It's long, too long and looks longer ... but it probably isn't any longer than usual. Except for now ... as I've put this extra bit in!!!!!

How are you?

Multiple choice, perhaps:
- ▶ Fair to Middling (Yorkshire term but not its origin, apparently (‿|‿) X1)
- ▶ Ask my psychiatrist.
- ▶ Not bad, until you asked and sent round another one of your effing emails!!!!
- ▶ None of the above. Insert your own response ... 🐾

Thanks for asking me, BTW!!! I'm 'splendid.' Well, not really. Somebody stole my antidepressants. Whoever they are, I hope they are happy! 😅

In this Week's Issue –

- ▶ Lockdown Easing – Including McaDees and Ikea.
- ▶ Around the World …
  - » Sweden … Herd Immunity. Experiment Failed?
  - » Hong Kong/Minneapolis, USA
  - » No(r)way … Slip Sliding Away
- ▶ Sex in the City (Well, House/Garden). Are You Lucky and Getting it? Be Careful Where You Dooooooooooooo It!!!! To be said in the style of legend Rik Mayall, if you can?!
- ▶ Sequels … Survey Results and a new one - Favourite/Best Kids TV Programme 'When Young' (Just Your Number 1). I might have given mine away in this email.
- ▶ Puzzles – Below. Easy or Hard. You tell me? 👬 Quiz … attached. 👬 Also starting next week - 'Items for Sale' Section. Starting with: 'Broken quiz machine, £10. No questions asked' … and a 'TV (for the same price) with bust volume knob' … 'You can't turn THAT down!' 😂

Lockdown Easing

McDonalds – I have just driven past, and they are queuing out into the road. Wow!!! That should help with the obesity issue and putting on weight is supposed to be a CV factor!? I went in, and some people were being quite rude, but the staff hit back by not putting any coke in their drinks ... Just ice was served!! 😆

Ikea – Perhaps you should make up your own jokes here? 😆

Ikea have now opened again, with queues around the block. Probably to buy stuff you don't need!! I am not a fan, and I have only ever been to Ikea twice (‿|‿) **X2**.

However, I do have a soft spot for the place as all my kids were conceived in an Ikea bed, which is ridiculous as those showrooms are so well lit. 😆

I did buy (genuinely, Steve?) some Ikea furniture that lasted 30 years; only because I didn't assemble it until I'd had it for 29, though!! 😆

Around the World

Hong Kong (HK) - I suppose Ikea could be likened to Hong Kong atm, as there is no peaceful assembly. Given CV, should HK request the services of Hong Kong Fluey to fight the pandemic? 😆 (See the end of this edition)

The one thing to say about the situation in HK is, would the Govt be offering such a repatriation deal if it was elsewhere in the world? Even if it had similar UK past links? I think not!!!

I still welcome the move, however, as the Beijing Govt

is a bit like my mam. When you go 'round for a cuppa, you only ever see the nice China!! 😂

I don't think I'll risk Ikea again soon, though, as it's complete chaos even at quiet times. But if YOU do go, make sure you do what China and American Police do regularly - Get up early, in order to beat the crowds!!!

Sweden and all about 'Herd Immunity' - or Was it Just 'Heard About Immunity'?!

I can't deny that Ikea is a success, but another Swedish experiment on Herd Immunity has failed. Luckily, we didn't carry on following them and jumped ship when we did.

https://www.wired.co.uk/article/sweden-coronavirus-herd-immunity

No(r)Way!!!! Also this week, some news away from Covid from the coast of Sweden's Scandinavian neighbour. Landslide sweeps houses (and dog) into the sea.

https://news.sky.com/story/norway-landslide-sweeps-dog-and-eight-houses-into-sea-12001446

Sex in the City (English Cities, not Scotland?)

Back to the UK. Lockdown measures have now been relaxed in visiting others' property. You can now go around to friends and relatives, have socially distanced barbeques, and even go to the toilet (not in Scotland). No toilet humour here as I decided to make this a crap joke-free zone/line??!!

Sex in the Basement, Bedroom or Attic ... is wrong on so many levels!!!!

Releasing some of the lockdown measures has created a rather strange anomaly ... it is NOW against the law to have sex in someone else's house, but you CAN 'do it' in the garden (as this is only advised against). So, getting down and dirty with your hoes is ok!

SO, sex is not the answer. Sex is the question. "Yes," is the answer. But only in the garden. This could still fall foul of other (privacy) laws if in open view, of course!!!!

'Filum' Sequels

Thanks for all your responses. It was a lot 'closer' at the top of the list than I would have thought.

The results are:
1 ... Aliens
2 ... Godfather Part 2
3 ... Toy Story 2/Empire Strikes Back. I listed Toy Story 2 first as, if I'd gone for the Transferable Voting System, it would have edged it on a recount!!!

Other Responses

Almost on the list was Rita, Sue and Bob Too!!! Remarkably, it was mentioned (comically, I think) by two of the first three people who replied.

Other options were the sequels to Cockerone, Mange One and Timbuk One. See https://www.youtube.com/watch?v=2pPMAaLo_UA from Milton Jones on Mock the Week (I can't even start to pretend this is my material) (‿|‿) **X3**

A list of all nominations can be found in (‿|‿) **X4**. When compared with 'Empire' Film Magazine list (‿|‿) **X5**, it is very similar. So it looks like we are quite representative. https://www.empireonline.com/movies/features/50greatestsequels/.

New Survey

Best Kids TV Show when you were growing up (or now, if you are still watching!)? Your Fave/Top 1 only!!!!!!! 👫

TV/Films

'Chernobyl' Fallout (Why Russians Wear Underpants) 😂

Speaking of nominations (a seamless segue into other film news this week!!), Chernobyl - starring Obi-Wan Chernobi (sorry!!) - received 14 nominations and got a big three thumbs up from BAFTA. See below. So many nominations, but you can still count them on the fingers of one Chernobyl hand. 😂

https://www.hollywoodreporter.com/news/2020-bafta-tv-awards-nominations-chernobyl-dominates-1297142#:~:text=Chernobyl%20leads%20the%20pack%20of,both%20Fleabag%20and%20Girl%2FHaji.

♫ Stevie's Puuuuuzzles of the Week ♫

Easy, Medium or Hard? … **You tell me!** 🧑‍🤝‍🧑

- ▶ I purchased two cigars which together cost 1.10. One cost one pound more than the other. How much do they both cost individually?
- ▶ There is an electrician and a plumber standing in line for admission at a trade fair. One is the father of the other one's son. How come?
- ▶ A woman had two sons who were born in the same hour of the same day of the same year, but they were not twins. How could this be?
- ▶ What 5-letter word becomes shorter by adding two letters. 🧑‍🤝‍🧑

Quiz

That's enough 'thinking' for one week, Steve. Let's do the full quiz next week!!

Next week –

- ▶ Dentists are reopening (so stop looking down in the mouth) and finally a chance to unleash my deluge of dentist jokes. 'Brace' yourselves. 😄 Yes, I've already started.
- ▶ Quiz at your request!!!
- ▶ Survey Results. Top Kids TV

TV

Tuesday 9th, Man on a Wire. Sky Documentaries,

Build my Gallows High, 10.20 pm Sony Movie Classics.

All t' best, and stay safe.

Steve

(‿|‿) **X1 Fair to middling** describes something that is average or only slightly above average. The term is an American phrase, used as early as the 1820s. The term **fair to middling** originally referred to gradations of quality in cotton, sheep and other farm goods.

(‿|‿) **X2** I did go to Ikea and almost lost my kids on both occasions. 'I think that one might be true, Steve.' I couldn't put this in the above text because how would this then work with my kids being conceived in an Ikea bed?

(‿|‿) **X3** I did actually 'crop' it initially, but then when I attached the file, it was a 10mb file. I thought it a little bit OTT just to top up the 'gag,' and it's probably best to listen to the whole sketch anyway.

(‿|‿) **X4** Godfather Pt 2, Aliens, Toy Story, T2, Indiana Jones 3, Empire Strikes Back, Return of the Jedi, Rocky 2, Mad Max 2, Croc Dundee 2, Jaws 2, Naked Gun 2½, Manon De Source, After the Third Man, Austin Powers 2, Bourne 2/3 … I think I have them all.

(‿|‿) **X5** I actually thought the order was a bit unexpected, but it is very similar to Empire. Shows how average we are?!

https://www.empireonline.com/movies/
features/50greatestsequels/.

Indiana 3 is on our list, but not Indi 2 (even though 2 is higher in the above list attached than 3). In this regard, I think the Empire list has it wrong.

Issue No 12
Sunday 14th June 2020

Statute on Statues Edition

Headlines:
- ► Coronavirus: WHO warns against further lifting of lockdown in England
- ► Scooter and moped demand triples as commuters look to shun buses and trains

Hello ... or, perhaps, with events this week, I should say Stat Chu??!!!!! CCC attached as usual for your enjoyment and pleasure ... wherever you see the 😊 ... blah blah blah.

I know I won't get a response from my Russian wife to this salutation, though, as whenever I say hello to her, she always says 'Private'!!! (‿|‿) **X1** To be fair, however, in every Russian woman, there is another nicer little Russian woman trying to get out!! 😊

There's another Lockdown Landmark (oops, don't say 'Landmark') tomorrow. Is this the end, or at least the beginning of the end? As per the announcement of the latest CV news By Dom Raab.

https://www.gov.uk/government/speeches/foreign-secretarys-statement-on-coronavirus-covid-19-15-june-2020

In this Issue –
- ▶ Statute and Strategy on Statues and is Basil Fawlty Dead or Resurrected?
- ▶ Protests Continue, and Others to Be aware of –
  - » The Letter B
  - » Global Warming
  - » Highways England (HE) and Road Signs
- ▶ Quiz and Dentist jokes combined. Less is More!!
- ▶ Stevie's Puzzle of the Week
- ▶ Survey – Last Week's Results (Kids TV)
- ▶ Next Week - TV and Luuuuuuurve is (Back) in the Air for Estranged Couples
- ▶ Coming out of Lockdown - (Continue to) Support your Local Businesses
- ▶ (ᵕ|ᵕ)(ᵕ|ᵕ)(ᵕ|ᵕ)

What is the Statute on Statues, and What's On and Off TV?

The constantly moving strategy of what will happen to various statues around the country continues. The Edward Colston one is 'fished' out of Bristol Harbour, Churchill gets boxed, and Scouts 'be prepared' (BP) to protect Baden Powell (BP). So, BP or not to BP, that is the question! Whereas, to be a horse rider or not to be a horse rider, that is equestrian! 😄

Nelson's Column (no, I can't do that one in this family version) also becomes one of 78 monuments under attack in the Capital - that's Horatio of 2 in 156 😄

BBC and Fawlty Towers ... Don't Mention Detour !!!!

(Actually, a U-turn, but it doesn't rhyme with 'War.')

Speaking of dodgy (or not) structures, Fawlty Towers has now been reinstated by the BBC on Catch Up after pressure from John Cleese and others. Surely, even the chaotic mind of Basil Fawlty would have never thought to censure this show - even in the present climate!!

Protests Continue 'On the Dirty Streets,' Litter Rally

('literally' - can't be good if I need to explain it !!)

Some less incendiary protests (not as Black and White!!) for consideration -

► In the (Alphabet) Soup – We all (h)ate the second letter of the alphabet, so let's Boo B (or not to Boo B, that is the question). I see a pattern developing here!!) (‿|‿) X2
Personally, I really detest the second letter of the alphabet more than anything, SO much that I'm starting a protest group. Will you protest with me? Here's the chant, say it with me!
... BOOOOOOO Bs! ... BOOOOOOO Bs! ... BOOOOOOO Bs!!!!!!!!!!!!!!!

► Climate Change has taken a back seat (of an electric car) for the moment, but it will be recycled soon.

However, It's NOT okay to mock kids for protesting against global warming. Well, not in the 'current climate' anyway. Even if it is for the Greta Good. 😂

► UK Highways England (HE) Strange Signs – Finally, back home in the UK and with our very own Highways England (HE). I know construction work can be inconvenient, but surely as a protest, this tops it all … "End Road Work"? No point in protesting about it, and btw, exit signs are also on their way out. 😂

Jokes Quiz – Dentists …

Don't look so down in the mouth, I told you it was coming!

With no nitrous oxide to help, I thought I'd make it a little easier by linking crap jokes with a puzzle this week. Surely you know them all? Have a go -

► 1. Time at the dentists?
► 2. Similarities with false teeth and stars?
► 3. My award-winning dentist has this in his office?
► 4. Can you smell gas?
► 5. Now, most dentist's chairs go up and down, don't they? The one I was in went back and forwards. I thought 'This is unusual.' And the dentist said to me?

- ▶ 6. My dentist said, 'Say arghhh ...' Why?
- ▶ 7. Does your dentist tell fibs when going about his business?
- ▶ 8. What do dentists believe in when cleaning their teeth?
- ▶ 9. My dentist writes lots of these 'gags' and helps me realign badly positioned ones. What is his specific profession?

  The answers, if you need any, are at (‿|‿) X3.

Last Week's survey results

Your favourite Kids TV shows were:

- ▶ Hong Kong Phooey (I suspect I prompted that a bit or couldn't be bothered thinking and replied anyway)
- ▶ Pipkins
- ▶ Bagpuss

Other selected selections - Crackerjack, Battle of the Planet, Playschool, Jamie and the Magic Torch, Vision On, Batman and Spiderman, UFO, Thundercats, He-man, MASK, Scooby Doo, Care Bears (not sure if genuine), Star Fleet, Thunderbirds, Captain Caveman, Ivor the Engine, Blue Peter, The Wombles, Button Moon and Banana Splits.

♫ Stevie's Puuuuuzzles of the Week ♫

... just a quickie or 2!!

- I have two coins which total 30p. Since one of the coins is not 10p, what are the two coins?
- When can you add 2 to 11 and get 1 as the answer?

Next Week

- Luuuuuuurve is (Back) in the Air for Estranged Couples
- Coming Out of Lockdown. (Continue to) Support your Local Businesses

TV

- Bullitt, ITV4 Thursday at 10 pm

All t' best, and stay safe,

Steve

(‿|‿) **X1** "Privyet," pronounced Private is Russian for "hello."

(‿|‿) **X2** I do have a heart as I took lots of crap jokes out here, and they probably sit better at the bottom, anyway!!! An extract of part of the extraction on alphabet soup protests … 'I often protest to Noel at Xmas, and after eating four cans of Alphabet Soup, I do expect a massive vowel movement but if constipated may struggle to get a word out.' If I vomit it all back up, what will the word on the street be?

(‿|‿) **X3** Jokes Quiz on Dentists answers

- ► 1. 2:30 - Tooth hurty.
- ► 2. They both come out at night.
- ► 3. A little plaque.
- ► 4. It's okay; I've just farted.
- ► 5. Come out of that filing cabinet.
- ► 6. "My dog's died."
- ► 7. No, he tells the whole tooth and nothing but the tooth.
- ► 8. Their flossophy.
- ► 9. He's an Authordentist.

There's no Issue No 13 as it could be bad luck. Good luck for you!!!

Issue No 14

Goodbye Bilbo

Headlines:

- ▶ Reopened pubs in England may require drinkers to check in
- ▶ Libyan held over Reading multiple stabbing 'known to security services'

Leeds Utd Update – Cardiff 2-0 Leeds

Hi … CCC attached for you know what when you see the 😄 sign.

A 'quickie' (well, let's see!!!) issue for me this week and a reminder really of the original purpose of this newsletter/vehicle: an attempt for us all to keep in touch and not just for (my) Crap Jokes!!

I have been in touch with a few people this week. This has just helped to remind me that, even though restrictions are lifting, many people's circumstances are different. We don't necessarily find out exactly how people are feeling via FB, WhatsApp, etc., unless we speak to each other. Seriously, please keep in touch with me if you wish, but make a special effort to keep in touch with others as much as possible.

CONGRATS - Finally, Mega-Congratulations to Mr C

and Laura on the birth of their new baby!

In this Week's Issue –

- ▶ Happy Birthday to Stan Laurel (Clint Eastwood's grandad, perhaps? The hair looks similar?) See (‿|‿) X1
- ▶ Goodbye to Ian Holm (of Hobbit Fame)
- ▶ Sleep - are you getting Enough? (the Teaspoon challenge) See (‿|‿) X2. "At night, I can't sleep. In the morning, I can't wake up" … attributed to most people at some point recently!!!
- ▶ Football is Back – IT Equipment is still on furlough, though!!!
- ▶ Stevie's Puuuuuzzles (and Last Week's Answers) of the Week
- ▶ Next Week
- ▶ Lord Stevie of Horsforth!!!

Happy Birthday to Stan Laurel and Goodbye to Ian Holm (The Hobbit)

Stan Laurel would have been 130 this week. Stan, of Laurel and Hardy Fame, AND potentially the Grandad of Clint Eastwood (sic) – 'That's another fine mess, punk'!!! This reminds me, the missus often says, I can do the work of two men; unfortunately, that's Laurel and Hardy. 😆

One of their best is below - an extract from the Music Box!!

https://www.youtube.com/watch?v=Mx87FnFfS5g

Ian Holm, who played Bilbo in LOTR, sadly passed away this week at not a bad age of 88. Perhaps he should have held onto the 'ring' a bit longer!! As a coincidence, I've been dreaming about being the author of the Hobbit all week and muttering his name whilst pumping out the Z's - I've been Tolkein in my sleep!!! Only one Mordor for Ian to go through!!! 😂

https://www.express.co.uk/celebrity-news/1298227/Ian-Holm-dead-How-did-Ian-Holm-die-lord-of-the-rings-hobbit-cause-of-death-latest

Sleeping Problems ... Insomnia or Resisting a Rest? 😂

Speaking of sleep, the latest lockdown figures suggest that over 50% of us are having sleeping difficulties, and many are having much more vivid dreams or nightmares (see link below).

https://www.theguardian.com/lifeandstyle/2020/apr/23/coronavirus-dreams-what-could-they-mean

In lockdown, I've decided that all that tossing and turning all night should be considered exercise. 😂

It's hardly surprising, really, that we are having trouble given changes to working practices, anxiety over COVID-19 and, of course, lack of routine.

I have a condition (like many) that makes me eat when I can't sleep; I call it insom-nom-nom-nom-nom-nomnia!" 😂

At least football is back (whether you like it or not - see below), which might return some normality and routine to lives. There is also news that many furloughed workers are going to get paid for being part of a study at the sleep clinic (sic) – it should be their dream job! 😂

To be fair, sleep is my favourite thing in the world. It's the reason I get up in the morning. 😂

Football is Back!!!!!!!!!!!!!

A good day for Leeds yesterday (even though they didn't play), given other results, but not so good today against Cardiff. Nuff said!!

Routine is good, however, and perhaps we can all agree that the return of football is good. Controversy wasn't far away as the first game caused issues because Hawkeye appeared to be still on furlough!!! Not giving a certain goal to Sheffield United against Villa!

See also below for Puzzle of the Week on football (sort of).

Stevie's Football Nickname. My nickname from teammates playing football for many years (was it really, Steve?) was Gandalf because ... **Well, you work it out!!!** 👥 (‿|‿) X3.

x

🎵 Stevie's Puuuuuzzles
(and Last Week's Answers) of the Week 🎵👥

… just a quickie or 2!!

► What ship has never arrived in the Ports of
Liverpool?
… I'd better do this one while I still can!!!! 😄
(⌣|⌣) X4

► Even if they are starving, natives living in parts
of the Artic will never eat a Penguin's egg. Why
not? And it's nothing to do with can't get the
wrappers off. That's why don't polar bears eat
penguins!!

Last Week's Answers:

► I have two coins which total 30p. Since one of
the coins is not 10p, what are the two coins?
A 10p and a 20p!!!! One of you suggested it
was half a crown and a shilling, pre-1971. So,
perhaps, two credible answers, but one is a
little 'easier' than the other!!!!

► When can you add 2 to 11 and get 1 as the
answer? A clock.

Next Week –

► Routine – What's worked in lockdown for you
and what hasn't? Your best and your worst!!!!!!!!
Let me know. 👥

► Out of Lockdown - (Continue to) Support your Local Businesses. I left it out deliberately this week as there might be some news about pubs by then.

TV

► - 12 Angry Men, TCM, Friday at 7.15. A classic. If never seen, it is worth watching, or again if have (seen).

All t' best, and stay safe.

Steve

AKA Lord Parker of Horsforth (following my Daughter's Father's Day Pressie … see following photo)

(◡|◡) **X1** https://www.theguardian.com/film/ filmblog/2009/jan/05/clint-eastwood-stan-laurel

(◡|◡) **X2** https://www.mirror.co.uk/news/weird- news/simple-metal-spoon-test-tell-9119829

(◡|◡) **X3** Thou Shall Not Pass … and now I have the beard as well!!!

(◡|◡) **X4** The Premier 'Ship' and I can still say it after tonight's results.

LORD STEVEN JEFFREY PARKER

THIS CERTIFICATE ASSERTS THE LEGAL RIGHT TO ASSUME THE HONORIFIC
TITLE LORD STEVEN JEFFREY PARKER OF HOUGUN MANOR. FURTHERMORE,
LORD STEVEN JEFFREY PARKER SHALL BE ASSIGNED DEDICATED LAND
WITHIN THE HOUGUN MANOR ESTATE, CUMBRIA, ENGLAND. THE
ASSIGNMENT NUMBER IS PS168-93820-1. THE ASSIGNOR IS ENYSEN
(LONDON) LTD (COMPANY NUMBER 09044078) AND DULY REGISTERED AND
VALIDLY EXISTING UNDER THE LAWS OF ENGLAND. THE VALIDITY,
INTERPRETATION AND IMPLEMENTATION OF THE ASSIGNMENT SHALL BE
GOVERNED BY THE LAWS OF THE UNITED KINGDOM OF GREAT BRITAIN
AND NORTHERN IRELAND.

Issue No 15
Sunday 28th June 2020

Pubs to Reopen!!!!

Headlines:

► Relationship between No 10 and Mark Sedwill was no longer tenable

► Global report: COVID-19 cases exceed 10m as anxieties rise over US

Sat 27th Leeds 3-0 Fulham

Hi … CCC attached for you know what when you see 😄. A little earlier this week (upon request).

Lockdown Highs and Blues

How are you? As we come out of (initial) lockdown, how has it been for you? **Please have a think and let me know your best and worst 'thing' or routine/habit in lockdown.** 👀

For the record, mine are –

► GOOD - I do go jogging occasionally (although I still hate it and am not getting much better). I do clean my teeth more (genuinely). For the last three weeks, I've been jogging a mile a day. The only problem is, I don't know where I am now. 😄

► BAD – Sleep patterns. Some nights, I can't find a comfortable position to sleep and yet, in the morning, every position is fine. 😂 I also watch TV too much, especially the news and, now it's back, football.

Let me know yours, please. 🏃 Obviously, I will only use them generically.

In this Week's Issue -

► Good News Bear Boris
► (About) Time Gentlemen, Please? Pubs Reopen - Unlockkkkk and Ordeerrrrrr!!!
► Happy Birthday to Me (again!!!)
► Life's a Beach
► Puzzle of the Week
► Next Week

Boris – The Good News Bear

Once again, there was some good news (for some) this week, so buoyant Boris (Mr Johnson) bounced up to the front of the Daily Briefing to announce there would be a further release of lockdown.

Pubs Reopen - Unlock (Lockdown) and Order (some beer) … or is it Orderrrrr and Unlockkkk …?

John Bercow's (The Speaker of the House) Best Bellows!!!!

See https://www.youtube.com/watch?v=dIodwVeS818

Yes, pubs are set to reopen on Independence (Brewers) Day (4th July). Given that Lockdown Day was on my Official Birthday (23rd March), it's only fair that we kick everything off with a celebration for my quarter B'day (23rd June) on Tuesday last week!

Will We Rush to the Local?

Is it about 'Time, Gentlemen, please' **or** is it too early? Believe it (or not?), I don't think I'll be rushing into my nearest pub on the 4th of July as, given the lag (in data), we might be doing everything a bit quick.

It is only a five-minute walk from my house to my local pub. And yet it's a 35-minute walk from the pub to my house. The difference is staggering!

The last time I was in the pub, someone said I could get the bus back home … but I think I'd be too drunk to drive that as well!!

Another 'seamless' segue into the next bit …

The Beach Boys walk into a bar …

"Round?"
"Round?"
"Get a round"
"I get a round?"
"Get a round …"

Life's A Beach!

As lockdown is lifted, a major Incident was reported in

Bournemouth as ½ a million (double the south coast town's population) people flocked like seagulls to the beach. On the news, there were bizarre scenes and interviews. In particular, one on the Six O'clock News, with someone who said, 'The scenes are crazy and a second wave is inevitable.' All of this, whilst standing in the middle of the chaos!!! The phrase, 'you are not **in** traffic, you **are** traffic,' springs to mind.

I love the beach but have not been recently. Long time no sea. 😎

Before the last wave, I was at the seasedi (See (‿|‿) **X1**), but I couldn't decide between the sand and the sea. You could say, 'it was 'tide.' Anyway, I just ended up throwing pebbles in the water. Which is a shame as my wife loved that dog! 😎 As he was swept out to sea, though, he was still doing magic tricks. After all, he was a Labracadabrador 😎, but he couldn't magic his way out of that!

Speaking of the wife and the beach, I should introduce her and tell you a little about what she does. It's really tricky to say what my wife does for a living, though – as she sells sea shells on the sea shore. 😎

🎵 Stevie's Puuuuuzzles
(and Last Week's Answers) of the Week 🎵 👥

... just a quickie or 2!!

- Grammar – Which is correct, the 'yolk of the egg are white,' OR the 'yolk of the eggs is white'?
- Maths – If you divide 30 by a half and add ten, what is the answer?

Last Week's Answers

- What ship has never arrived in the Ports of Liverpool … The Premier Ship. 😏 As I said, I can't use it anymore now they have won the title.
- Even if they are starving, natives living in parts of the Artic will never eat a Penguin's egg. Why not?

  Answer … **There are NO penguins in the Artic!!**

Next Week –

- Routine – What's worked in lockdown for you and what hasn't? Your best and your worst. Send me your thoughts. 🧐
- TV - Casablanca TCM, 7 pm, Tuesday. A classic, but I don't believe the best of Bogey!?

All t' best, and stay safe.

Steve

(◡│◡) **X1** Don't forget the golden rule: 'i before e, except after sea'!!!!

Issue No 16

MONDAY 6TH JULY 2020

Air Bridge Chaos

Headlines:

- ► County lines gangs disguised drug couriers as key workers during coronavirus lockdown
- ► Chancellor under pressure to boost financial support as job crisis looms

Sat 4th July Blackburn 1-3 Leeds

Hi … CCC attached for you know what when you see the 😀 sign. A little earlier this week (upon request).

Apologies for the delay and to those who have not received recent issues … perhaps you are the lucky ones!!!!!!!

Headlines - pubs are finally open. Leicester is in lockdown after a resurgence … is it Boo Hoo for them?! (‿|‿) **X1,** and is it Whack-a-Mole or Guacamole? Genuinely, I only just realised it was the former - a reference to concentrating on a particular area with Covid measures and not complete gobbledegook!!!!

In this Week's Issue –

- ► The Good, the Bad and the Ugly of Lockdown – drafted, coincidentally, before today's death of Ennio Morricone https://www.bbc.co.uk/news/entertainment-arts-19626787

- ▶ Samuel Pepys Diary Quote!! 1665
- ▶ Holiday Destinations Released and 'Air Bridge' Chaos. Are Air Bridges like Air Guitars - do they actually exist?
- ▶ Schools' Bigger Bubbles and Less (sorry, fewer) Lessons for Kids
- ▶ PM's Reverse Sweep - Good for Local Cricket?
- ▶ Puzzles of the Week
- ▶ Next Week - Beethoven and My Trip to his Grave

The Good, the Bad and the Ugly of Lockdown

Thanks for all your input/returns into Lockdown Highs and Blues. **Please keep them coming, and I'll do a full(er) return next week.** 👬

Here's a quick review of those received so far:

- ▶ Good – Time to reflect, read more, wear comfy clothes and listen to music.
- ▶ Bad – Disturbed sleep, not seeing friends and family, anxiety about CV and everything!
- ▶ Some said Good/Bad – Wildlife, Exercise and putting weight on or taking it off!!
- ▶ Exercise - I've (genuinely) been doing some Press-Ups in lockdown, but please, will someone tell me how your chest is supposed

to hit the ground first (and not my stomach) before pushing up!?!

▶ Wildlife – (as above) again, both good and bad for some. It is nice to see more of nature, but it is also becoming a nuisance. Our good friend Sean Connery has often been a big advocate of protecting wildlife, but his chant of 'Shave the Wildlife' might have been misunderstood!!! An enormous black bird is on my lawn every morning and hardly moves, almost as if it is stuck there - it must be a Velcrow! 😄

Routine can be good or bad

The one thing most agreed was that getting into a routine can be very good BUT also very bad if it's the wrong type. So, start making nice clothes for nuns as it's good habit forming. 😄

I became a bit addicted to injecting bleach after Trump's recent announcement … but I'm clean now! 😄

Samuel Pepys' Diary

Many of you may have seen the quote circulating that seems very apt for this moment in time …

'The taverns are fair full of gadabouts making merry this eve. And though I may press my face against the window like an urchin at a confectioner's, I am tempted not by the sweetmeats within. A dram in exchange for the pox is an ill bargain indeed.' (‿|‿) **X2**

Some Holidays Are Back on the Agenda

The UK travel quarantine rules have been explained, and a full list of countries has been announced ... see https://www.bbc.co.uk/news/business-53261752

Air Bridge – Terminal Illness!! Air (Guitar) Bridges - Do They Actually exist??!!

In another U-turn, well, it would have been, if anybody knew what the policy was in the first place – I'm afraid, this error-plane never got off the ground!! 😅

I went to the airport last week to see if I could find out what was going on. I went up to the desk going 'cluck, cluck, cluck, cluck'. The woman said to me, 'Sorry, sir, this is the 'check-in' desk.' 😅

Don't you just hate that situation when you're picking up your bags at the airport, and everyone's luggage is better than yours?

For me, it's just the worst-case scenario!! 😅

👬 Finally, does anyone know why when mail goes by sea it's called "CARgo" and yet when mail goes by land it's called a "SHIPment"?! 👬

School's Return with Bigger Bubbles and Less (sorry, fewer) Lessons.

As ALL(?) pupils are set to go back in September with bigger bubbles (I'll try not to burst them for the kids!!), you may have seen the sign created by the Ed Sec Gavin Williams (below) to encourage pupils, parents and teachers alike to back his plans!!!

PM – Local Cricket Can Resume (we think?)

Boris Johnson makes another 'slip' and takes up a 'silly point' (‿|‿) **X3** on cricket but was told he was speaking 'palpable nonsense' (see following link - https://www.theguardian.com/sport/2020/jul/03/palpable-nonsense-boris-johnson-criticised-for-latest-cricket-declaration).

Anyway, he finally dashed for 'deep cover' before doing another 'reverse sweep/U-Turn' on the resumption of local cricket. Not the first time (or last), he's hit his own wicket and was ordered back to the pavilion. 😂

Puzzle of the Week

🎵 Stevie's Puuuuuzzles
(and Last Week's Answers) of the Week 🎵👥

… on request, these are a little harder perhaps (without the lateral 'twist').

- ► There are two plastic jugs filled with water. How could you put all of this water into a barrel, without using the jugs or any dividers, and still tell which water came from which jug?
- ► If I am 80cm plus half my own height, how tall am I?

Last Week's Answers

- ► 'easy(ish)' as long as you spotted the Lateral thinking aspect.
- ► Grammar (not really was it) – Which is correct, the 'yolk of the egg are white,' OR the 'yolk of

the eggs is white'? YOLK IS YELLOW!!!!

▶ Maths – If you divide 30 by a half and add ten, what is the answer? By a half, not in half … so answer 70.

Next Week –

▶ TV/Radio – Monday – Being Beethoven, BBC4. 250 years celebration. I've actually been to Beethoven's Grave. He actually had three burials (sic) - see (‿|‿) X4 for my account.

▶ TV … Hacksaw Ridge C5, Tuesday 10 pm. It's a bit bloody, but made with incredible direction and based on a true story.

All t' best, and stay safe.

Steve

(‿|‿) **X1** Not mocking Leicester with 'fake tears' as BooHoo is the clothing factory where the outbreak is centred. https://www.theguardian.com/uk-news/2020/jul/04/boohoo-booms-leicester-garment-factories-linked-lockdown

(‿|‿) **X2** Unfortunately, Pepys, it is not!!!!!

(‿|‿) **X3** For those not familiar with cricket fielding positions, see https://en.wikipedia.org/wiki/Fielding_(cricket)#:~:text=These%20positions%20include%20Slip%20(often,Leg%20gully%3B%20the%20short%20and including the 'silly positions' of silly point, mid-on and mid-off. So-called, I assume, as they are so close to the bat!!!

(‿|‿) **X4** Beethoven – my account of my visit to Beethoven's grave is below ...

When I visited his grave, I was walking through the cemetery and heard some strange noise coming from the area where Beethoven was buried. Startled, I ran

and got the priest to come and listen to it. The priest bent close to the grave and heard some faint, unrecognisable music coming from the grave. Frightened, the priest ran and got the town magistrate.

When the magistrate arrived, he bent his ear to the grave, listened for a moment, and said, "Ah, yes, that's Beethoven's Ninth Symphony, being played backwards."

He listened a while longer and said, "There's the Eighth Symphony, and it's backwards, too. Most puzzling." So the magistrate kept listening; "There's the Seventh ... the Sixth ... the Fifth.."

Suddenly the realisation of what was happening dawned on the magistrate. He stood up and announced to the crowd that had gathered in the cemetery, "My fellow citizens, there's nothing to worry about. It's just Beethoven decomposing."

Issue No 17

Monday 13th July 2020

Another Leeds' Legend, Jack Charlton, Dies

Headlines:

► Dominic Cummings urged to release data to disprove claim of second lockdown trip

Hi … CCC attached for you know what when you see the 😁 sign or whenever.

Jack Charlton RIP

As Leeds make another step towards the Premier League (as we all hope!!), I start again this week with some sad news. Jack Charlton, the Leeds Utd Legend and World Cup winner, passed away a few days ago. Tributes have been pouring in for 'Big Jack' – Yorkshire's favourite Geordie and Ireland's favourite Englishman. He played over 700 times, over 23 years AND for one club. That won't happen again in football.

Mi Mam and Big Jack!!!

Related and continuing with being serious (honest, for once). As already mentioned to some, I've just been speaking to mi mam. She was in tears when I phoned. I was worried at first, until she said, 'You didn't tell me that Big Jack had died!!!' She was at Elland Road watching Big Jack and Leeds straight after her wedding in 1962, before going on honeymoon.

In this Week's Issue –

- ▶ Lockdown Ups and Downs
- ▶ WFH in Barbados, perhaps
- ▶ My Sick Crow (again)
- ▶ Mask Wearing
- ▶ Gyms Open. We Don't Go. We Keep Paying. The End!!!!!
- ▶ Happy 1st AND 2nd Anniversary to Steve!!!
- ▶ Puzzles of the Week and Last Week's Answers
- ▶ Next week's TV etc

Lockdown Blues

Thanks for your continuing responses to what works (and not) in lockdown. Here are a few final entries:

- ▶ Good – No commuting and wearing comfy clothes
- ▶ Bad – No dentists available. Might not have needed (yet), but the fear of needing and not being available (if we do).

Good and BAD. Finally, as you can see from my picture attached. I've finally grown a decent beard but at a cost. It's really taken its toll!!!!!! Has Santa/Xmas arrived early? 😂

WFH in Barbados, perhaps!!!

As many of us continue to work from home and as it becomes the 'new norm,' perhaps others have seen this as an opportunity to continue to do so in warmer climes.

See https://www.bbc.co.uk/news/topics/cp7r8vgl2jxt/barbados

- ► New WFH regime is now linked to social class –
  - » Working-class – can't work at home
  - » Middle-class – can work at home
  - » Upper-class – others work at your home

As a 'middle-class first-world citizen,' I still feel I know just as much about working in a sweatshop in China as the children themselves. After all, I've walked a mile in their shoes. 😊

Sick Crow - A Lost Caws

Apologies from last week; the crow I mentioned was not stuck there at all (velcrow) but was actually dead (a lost caws). It must have died of Corvid/Cawvid (delete as you wish (‿|‿) **X1**). There you go, two high/lowbrow jokes combined. 😂 😂 Or high/lowcrow, perhaps. That's enough crow jokes, eh, Steve!!!??

Okay, but just to finish. When I went to bury it, I noticed there were a few crows camping at the end of the garden. I concluded it was murder within tent (‿|‿) **X2** 😂

Mask Wearing

Breaking news ... 'Trump seen in mask wearing shocker' - see (mis-steak) attached and 'next week' below.

Confusion continues over the likely rules (or otherwise) on face masks and when we should (or not) be wearing them in shops, pubs, etc.

For instance, I went to the bank today, and there were a couple of men in masks. You could tell everyone's anxiety increased, BUT we were all relieved, however, when they said they were just there to rob the bank! 😂

At home, the missus said I should put the mask on every time I leave the house - so I always do. But I think she is sick of that stupid movie now. 😂

244

I did start using a sleeping mask instead to protect from Covid, but it went missing. I'll not rest until I find it. 😄

Finally, I started wearing woman's panties for a face mask instead. Well, I have ever since my wife found them in the glove box. 😄

Gyms, etc.

Opening at a place near you soon????

Will we have to wear masks at the gym? I decided to cancel my membership as me and the wife just don't have the energy to go anymore. I did give them a 'too weak' notice, though. I had to break it off as we were just not working out!!!! 😄

Do it Yourself at Home?

As mentioned last week, I've been doing press-ups in lockdown (and, previously, very slow jogging), but I've also been doing sit-ups. I feel I'm atoning for my eating sins by doing as many sit-ups a day as possible - or 'Ab Solution' as I like to call it!!! 😄

This fitness regime has helped me to do something I'll be discussing next week – 'Yachting in Italy, Spain and Monaco' and I'm only allowed to steer with my stomach muscles. Yes, it's a new feature… 'Abseiling in the Med.' 😄

Congratulations - Happy Anniversary to Steve!!!

Speaking of working out, I'd not be doing any of this

if not for my 1st and 2nd Anniversary this week ('work out' yersen!!). A clue (?), I have socks and pants older than my hips. Not many can say that!!! (‿|‿) X3

♫ Stevie's Puuuuuzzles
(and Last Week's Answers) of the Week ♫

▶ What is the third hand of a watch called?
▶ Before cholesterol concerns, people used to believe that –
   » MNXRLT4U (‿|‿) X4

Last Week's Answers

▶ There are two plastic jugs filled with water. How could you put all of this water into a barrel, without using the jugs or any dividers, and still tell which water came from which jug?
   Freeze the water and then put it in.
▶ If I am 80cm plus half my own height, how tall am I?
   200cm.

Next Week –
▶ The Govt Great Cash Giveaway Incentive (although some Primark/William Hill are giving it back!!!) and the Eating out with 50% off. Well, we can do that now on a number of cards, anyway ... e.g. – Tastecard.

TV/Radio
- ▶ Braveheart, Sony Movies Fri 17th 9 pm.
- ▶ Being Beethoven continues (on now) BBC 4.

All t' best, and stay safe.

Steve

(⌣|⌣) **X1** https://en.wikipedia.org/wiki/Corvidae and caw is the sound.

(⌣|⌣) **X2** Murder is the term for a gathering of crows.

(⌣|⌣) **X3** Anniversaries (1 year and 2 year) of having hips replaced (sic).

(⌣|⌣) **X4** If you have seen (m)any Two Ronnies' Sketches, it might help.

Issue No 18

Monday 20th July 2020

Leeds Are Champions Edition

Headlines:

- ▶ Senior doctors warn second coronavirus wave could 'devastate' NHS
- ▶ Coronavirus: Boris Johnson insists he can avoid second England-wide lockdown

LEEDS ARE CHAMPIONS EDITION!!!!!!!!!!!!!

CCC is attached for when you see this sign. 😄

Hi,

Obviously, there is only one way to 'kick off' this week. Leeds have been promoted back to the Premier League for the first time in 16 years ... AND, as champions! Mad celebrations erupted, although they did it without kicking a ball. When 'Leeds' did play, we came from behind to thrash Derby, even though only half the team were available (missing/hungover). Derby gave Leeds a 'Guard of Honour' as well. Hope that didn't stick in 'Craw' too much!!!! Congrats to Bielsa, all the lads and everyone associated with the club.

What a weekend! Promoted on Friday, Champions on Saturday, Slaughter Derby Sunday.

As you can imagine, there was lots of partying over the weekend (not all of which was socially distanced), so you could say that the 'city went missing.' Police said, 'They had no Leeds'!!! 😄

One Gag Bites the Dust!!!

And one gag that is no more and can be finally put to bed …

What does a Leeds United fan do when his team wins the Championship?

He turns off the PlayStation … X😄X Off the list now for everyone!!??

This makes up for the last 16 years and especially the disappointment of last year that was soul-destroying and like crushing a can of coke - it was soda pressing! 😄

In this Week's Issue –

- ▶ Bad Archer
- ▶ Butterfly Count – on a Wing and a Prayer
- ▶ Caption Comp – NEW FEATURE
- ▶ Stevie's Puzzles of the Week and Last Week's Answers
- ▶ Next Week

Cricket - Bad (Jofra) Archer – Aimed at Sky and Missed 😄

In other sports news this week, England level the series against the Windies. Jofra Archer is available for the 3rd Test after putting at risk the whole Test Series (and more) by going on an unauthorised trip to his parents. He was fined and had to isolate.

I'm sure you all know the difference between a bad archer and a constipated owl: one shoots but can't hit, and the other hoots but can't … 😄

Butterfly Count

Speaking of beautiful things soaring (as in Leeds Utd), you may have seen this (link below). All hands/ wings needed, and it's easy to join in. In addition, with lockdown, anxiety, etc., it might be a perfect time to do so.

https://bigbutterflycount.butterfly-conservation.org/

There are no jokes about throwing margarine alternatives out of the window today … to see butterfly. 😄

An ex-girlfriend of mine was very involved in such activities and spent hours every day counting (butterflies) … I wonder what she's up to now? 😄

Caption Competition – New Feature 🖼️

My daughter has reworked and updated a drawing some of you may recall from many years ago. Don't worry, it won't be a picture/caricature of me every week!!!!

Let me know your 'wording' for the caption by **noon on Saturday.** There is a prize for the best entry.

🎵 Stevie's Puuuuuzzles (and Last Week's Answers) of the Week 🎵 📇

- ▶ What can go up a chimney down but not down a chimney up?
- ▶ You measure my life in hours, and I serve you by expiring. I'm quick when I'm thin and slow when I'm fat. The wind is my enemy. What am I?

Last Week's Answers

- ▶ What is the third hand of a watch called?
  Obviously, the 3rd hand is called the second hand.
- ▶ Before cholesterol concerns, people used to believe that MNXRLT4U.
  Ham and Eggs are Healthy for you.

Next Week's TV

- ► Eddie the Eagle, Film 4. 6.55 pm Tuesday 21
- ► The Shining 10.50 pm BBC1

All t' best and stay safe.

Steve

(‿|‿) X1 ... **No bottoms this week. First time ever?!**

Issue No 18A

VERSION (Transitioning Edition)

Hi,

In the words of Corporal Jones, **Don't Panic ... Don't Panic ... Don't Panic ...!** https://www.youtube.com/watch?v=nRolOtdvqyg.

Everything is okay, and the next (full) SFTWS version will be out soon (you will be glad to hear!!!). Thanks for all your messages of concern!!

Apologies for the delay but given that we are slowly moving out of lockdown, I felt it was the right time to go Bi-Weekly (well, there are so many Gender/Orientations out there now to choose from), so this is a transitional edition!!!

The next one is drafted and ready to go, so it should be published this weekend under the new regime. Hopefully, the gags and topics won't be that out of date by then (as if that matters, Steve!!!).

In this Issue –
- ▶ The Only News Is there Is no News!!!
- ▶ Transitional Edition 18A - see above.
- ▶ No Puzzles
- ▶ No Quizzes
- ▶ Next week - First Bi-weekly Edition

> » Caption Comp Results … so there is still time to enter
> » Spanish Hols
> » Keep fit and …
> » More on the Big Masks Debate!!!

Take care and stay safe!!!!!

Steve
No Bottoms (⊡|⊡)

Issue No 19

MONDAY 3RD AUGUST 2020

Further Local Lockdowns

Headlines:

- ► Secrecy has harmed UK government's response to COVID-19 crisis, says top scientist
- ► COVID-19: government 'considers indoor mixing ban and M25 block' in England

22 July Leeds 4-0 Charlton - LEEDS GO UP
AS CHAMPIONS IN STYLE!!!

Hi … CCC for your use when you see the 😂 sign, or when you wish.

Headlines

There is no more on **football** this week, except to say it was great to watch the tension unfold recently on the last day(s) of the season and the Play-Offs, while Leeds were already secured in the Premier League.

There are further **local lockdowns** (esp. in North of England), but clarity on what we can and can't do is somewhat lacking. The best summary I can give is that you can only meet people indoors, as long as there is a card reader available to act as a chaperone in order to spend money. 😂

Russia Report. No news - and was old news by now anyway!? If there was nothing to report, why was it held back? Boris does have something in common with Russian dolls, though. Both are full of themselves. I Putin some effort to that joke. 😂

In this Week's Issue –

- ▶ Face Masks and Anomalies
- ▶ Spain - 🎵 We Aren't Goin' on a Summer Holiday!!! 🎵

- Caption Competition - Results

- ▶ Stevie's Puzzle(s) of the Week!!
- ▶ Next Week

Mask Debate and Other Anomalies –

Well, it is now law to wear facemasks in shops. We should have been doing this for months, perhaps? In Costa, all the Baristas are wearing them but calling them 'Coughy Filters.' 😂

One thing occurred to me. Do you need to wear a mask in the face mask shop when going to buy one?! Or what about if we go to the barbers for a shave?!

You may also recall recently I mentioned Shipments (on land) and yet Cargo (on Ships) is weird as well.

Other anomalies that I recall over the years are below. **Let me know yours.** 👥

- ▶ How does the man who drives the snow plough

get to work?

- If a tree falls in the forest, and nobody is around to hear it, does it make a sound and do the other trees laugh at it?
- How is it possible to draw a blank … perhaps next week's Caption Comp?
- Why do they call a women's prison a penal colony?
- Why does nobody have bulletproof pants?
- Why does the sun come up and go down when everything else goes up and comes down?
- Why is it called after dark when it's really after light?
- Why does the Lone Ranger always have Tonto with him? 😄

… Have you got any? 👥

🎵 **Spain - We're all NOT Going on a Summer Holiday!!!!** 🎵

Tough line by Govt, four months too late, perhaps??

Not many know that I met my wife while I was on a business trip in Spain. I said to her, "What are you doing here?" 😄

But, seriously, I was hoping to go back and get another tattoo this summer. People never believe me when I tell them that I got my first incredibly detailed tattoo in Spain. Nobody, of course, expects the Spanish ink

precision (‿|‿) **X1.**

Spain's infection rate has gone up recently, though. Even the King of Spain has been quarantined on his private jet. This means the Reign in Spain stays mainly in his plane. But his pet isn't in quarantine – as he can't leave his Catalonia.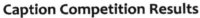

Finally, if he does get sick, he may have to Barf-a-lona!!

Caption Competition Results

The WINNER ... 'Better Latte than Never, by Mick M.' My daughter's entry also deserves a mention (especially given the drawing was produced by my other daughter). She said, 'The first is a realistic drawing of Dad by my sister and the other is when she wants summat!!'

🎵 Stevie's Puuuuuzzles
(and Last Week's Answers) of the Week. 🎵👥

- ▶ Which word is the odd one out … and why?
  Oriole, Orange, Month, Oil.
- ▶ Can you translate the following …
  YYURYYUBICURYY4ME?

Last Edition's Answers
- ▶ What can go up a chimney down but not down
  a chimney up?
  An umbrella.
- ▶ You measure my life in hours, and I serve you
  by expiring. I'm quick when I'm thin and slow
  when I'm fat. The wind is my enemy. What am I?
  A candle

Next Week
- ▶ Fitness Challenge and Eat Out to Help Out
- ▶ TV – Joker, Sky Premiere 8 pm Friday 7th. It
  completely polarises opinion, but it's worth a
  watch.

All t' best and stay safe.

Steve

(◡|◡) **X1** - There were plenty of options, so I did let you off lightly here.

▶ Quarantine in Spain, if I have a ball-point pen. The Spanish-Ink position!! AND there were many more in the locker!!

Issue No 20

MONDAY 17TH AUGUST 2020

Exam Chaos

Headlines:

► Dominic Cummings urged to release data to disprove claim of second lockdown trip

Hi

CCC – attached for your pleasure for use when you see the 😄 sign. Apologies to those who missed the recent announcement, but SFTWS is now bi-weekly!!!! And will be issued at the new 'Tea-time slot'!!!!

In this Issue –

► French Holiday Farce
► Exam Chaos. Report on Authorities ... Must Try Harder/Do Better!!!!
► Amazing Sport – Super Snooker
► Stevie's Puzzle(s) of the Week and Last Week's Answers!!
► Next Week
► (‿|‿)(‿|‿)(‿|‿)

French Holiday Farce

Following the last edition's news about Spain's quarantine, it is France's turn this week as the Govt announce the need for those returning from France to quarantine for two weeks. It's a shame they weren't as quick to impose such measures five months ago!!!

I was watching TV shows on the 75th Anniversary of VJ Day this weekend. Scenes from the English Channel were more like Dunkirk as Brits in France made a mad rush to grab some fast food (not snails, of course!!) and dash to the ferry. My mum's sister, who is on holiday there, and now stranded, is certainly one cross aunt. 😄

I said, 'Are you sure you need to come back immediately?' She just replied … 'Adieu.'

She is doing a tour of French Towns atm, doing impressions of Star Trek characters. 'Dunkirk?' I said. 'All of them,' she replied!! 😄

Anyway, for those having to scamper back from the French Riviera - it certainly wasn't Nice!! 😄

Exam Chaos – Must Do Better!!!!

The Sec of State for Education, Gavin Williams, couldn't pass a urine test, but the new algorithm to decide on students' marks is truly taking the pee!!

It's not just Archaeology students with their future in ruins or the Egotistical students who are appealing. 😄

The controversial algorithm has downgraded millions of students' marks and sent the 'clearings' and university enrolment system into meltdown.

People sitting the Pest Control Exam were most

annoyed as they have been swatting all through lockdown. 😊

Any more from you? 👥

This is set to be repeated with GCSEs (see below) although, at the time of 'going' to print,' an announcement was 'imminent' on a potential change of course/delay. I suspect it might involve a 'turn' based on that letter in the alphabet between 'T' and 'V.' 😊 See the following link.

https://www.theguardian.com/education/2020/aug/15/controversial-exams-algorithm-to-set-97-of-gcse-results

My Exam History – It isn't good. I failed a blood test once as I had too much blood in my alcohol stream. Perhaps Gavin Williamson has had one too many before coming up with his algorithm – you should never drink and derive. 😊

In another type of exam, I failed a prostate exam because I ran out of the room when the doctor's reply to my question, 'Where should I put my pants?' was, 'Over there, next to mine.' 😊 I wasn't expecting that!!

Don't be fooled either, as the digital examination does not involve any kind of electronic device and/or computer. 😊

My solution to most exams.

It's best just to eat all exam papers - and, eventually,

you will pass the test. 😄

Real Exam Answers

Some genuine exam answers are shown at the end of this issue (‿|‿) X1. You may have seen some of them before, but they are well worth a(nother) look.

What's your fave? 👥 Mine is probably the fibula one!!

Sport – Another weekend of amazing Sport – Super Snooker

Bayern beat Barcelona 8-2, and Man City are dumped out of the Champions League by Lyon. But to stay away from football, for once, I think snooker is worth highlighting this edition.

Ronnie (O'Sullivan) makes it a 6th world title (and 7 before book published), but the final was always going to be overshadowed by two amazing last-frame semi-final deciders that left all shocked and one player in tears. Watch it (again) if you get the chance on iPlayer/YouTube.

I played a lot of snooker in my youth and used to live on a diet of snooker balls. I once had to go to the Docs coz my stomach was killing me. The first thing he asked was about was my diet. I replied, "I eat red ones for breakfast. I eat the white and black for lunch. I eat blue and yellow for dinner. And a few more reds for supper, depending how hungry I am." "Yep, I see the problem," says the doctor. "You're not eating enough greens." 😄

Finally, who takes the second shot in a snooker game?
Find out after the break. 😄

🎵 Stevie's Puuuuuzzles of the Week 🎵👨‍🎤

This week, keeping with the themes above:
- ▶ France – The first French fry was not cooked in France, but where?
- ▶ Exams – I'm livid. I failed to remember how to write 1, 1000, 51, 6, and 500 as Roman numerals in my Latin exam. How come?
- ▶ Snooker – What is the highest break in snooker?

Easy, medium and very 'Tricky' answers on this one!! A drink on me if you get all three!!

Last Week's Answers
- ▶ Which word is the odd one out … and why? Oriole, Orange, Month, Oil.

Oil. Only word that can rhyme with another word.

- ▶ Can you translate the following … YYURYYUBICURYY4ME?

**Too Wise You Are, Too Wise You Be,
I See You Are Too Wise for Me.**

Next Week's TV and Films
- ▶ TV – BBC4 Tuesday 9 pm, The Yorkshire Ripper Files: A Very British Crime Story. Shown a few

years ago but well worth a(nother) watch - especially for those who lived through it.

► Films – Nocturnal Animals Friday 10 pm, Sony Movies

Next Edition - How are we coping with the lifting (or not) of lockdown?

All t' best and stay safe.

Steve

(‿|‿) **X1 Real Exam Answers**

3. Find x.

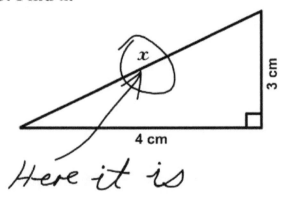

Here it is

Where was the American Declaration of Independence signed?

At the bottom.

CHECKING IN (Answer on your own and hand in to your instructor)

The water of the earth's oceans stores lots of heat. An engineer designed an ocean liner that would extract heat from the ocean's waters at $T_h = 10°C$ (283 K) and reject heat to the atmosphere at $T_1 = 20°C$ (293 K). He thought he had a good idea, but his boss fired him. Explain.

Because he slept with his boss' wife. —Jathun...

Oh dear!

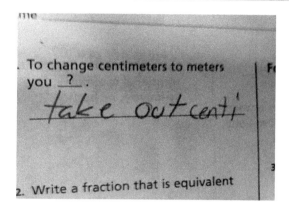

. To change centimeters to meters you __?__ .

take out centi

2. Write a fraction that is equivalent

3. what are the 2 types of sex cells?

+2   Eggs
      Sperm

4. During what stage do the chromosomes line up in the middle of the cell?

+0   it's a secret ← No way!

Explain the phrase 'free press'.

When your mum irons trousers for you.

269

▶ Miranda can't see anything when she looks down her microscope.

Suggest one reason why not

_____She is blind____ x Nice try!

🗇 Draw a picture of what you will look like in 100 years. In 100 years I will be_____years old!

10. The diagram below best illustrates
    a. Lamarck's theory of evolution.
    b. Darwin's theory of evolution.
    c. Malthus's principles.
    d. Lyell's theory about past changes.
    e. Giraffes are heartless creatures.

Name six animals which live specifically in the Arctic.

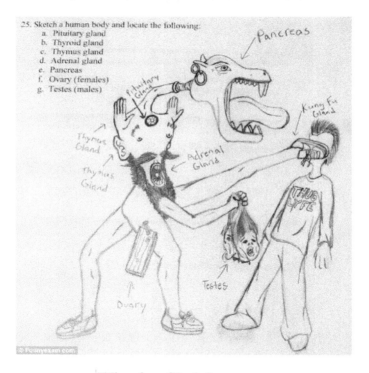

Two polar bears
~~Three~~ four Seals

What is a fibula?

A little lie

Joanna works in an office. Her computer is a stand-alone system. What is a stand-alone computer system?

It doesn't come with a chair

Assess Fashion House plc's choice to locate its factory near Birmingham. Is Birmingham the right location for this type of business?

No. People from Birmingham aren't very fashionable.

3. Name an angle complimentary to BDC:

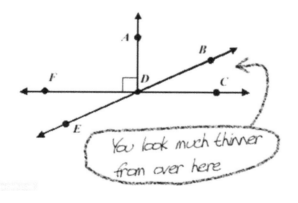

You look much thinner from over here

PETER

1.21

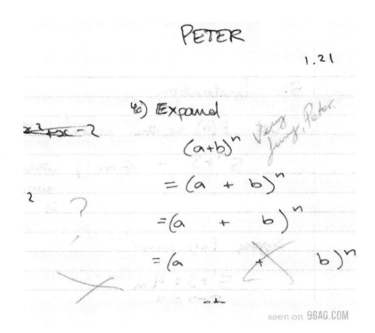

$\not{6}$) Expand

$(a+b)^n$ Very funny, Peter

$= (a + b)^n$

$= (a + b)^n$

$= (a \quad\quad b)^n$

Issue No 21
Tuesday 1st September 2020

Headlines:
- Marcus Rashford takes aim at child food poverty with new taskforce
- Gap between rich and poor pupils in England grows by 46% in a year

Hi All

Apologies for the delay, but I had some work to do over the BH Weekend!!!!!!!!!

'Well Done,' Chancellor!!

As Rishi's Din Din's Discount (or 'having a Rishi') ends, another two weeks have flown by. We will, of course, be paying all those freebies back in taxes shortly!!! Rishi became extremely constipated by eating out so much himself. He just couldn't even budge it. 😂

Feedback

Thanks, as always, for all the feedback (I'll not do my chicken pellet business joke, again … oops!!), but I'll reciprocate by saying thanks to all those who told me the definition of the word 'many' … it means a lot. 😂

Comic Cone Chortle (CCC)

A proper heading for once, rather than CCC – *attached for your pleasure for use when you see the* 😂 *sign.*

In this Week's Issue -
- ▶ Back to School – is the Chaos Over?!
- ▶ Gavin Williamson Remains in Post … Somehow
- ▶ American Elections – Marge Simpson Wades in
- ▶ Unbaaaalievable, Jeff!!!!
- ▶ Caption Competition Returns
- ▶ Stevie's Puzzle(s) of the Week!!
- ▶ Next Week

Back to School – Chaos continues? Who is the Dunce of the Class?!?!

As we all know, 'Those who can, do. Those who can't, teach.' Those who can't, become Secretary of State for Education – and Gavin Williamson is still there!!

He is so bad; every time he speaks, he gives me heartburn and indigestion, so when he does finally go, I'll be able to say, "I can't believe that Gaviscon!!" 😂

Perhaps, at best, I could say he is average … Is that 'mean?' 😂

Adverse Criticism and Algorithms

I'll spare you a gag revolving around the former Vice-President of the US of A tapping a beat out on a drum (⌣|⌣) X1.

As we know, this Govt doesn't want anything to do with bad headlines or negative numbers. In fact, they will stop at nothing to avoid the latter. 😂

However, algorithms continue to cause bad headlines,

with a few more on the way. Perhaps they should come up with an algorithm for everything atm and just base it on a game of Chase the Ace. 😂 (‿|‿) **X2**

American Elections

Just when you thought it couldn't get any stranger, the American Elections diverted us into left field when a Trump campaign adviser got into Twitter spat with Marge Simpson ...

https://www.theguardian.com/tv-and-radio/2020/aug/15/marge-simpson-trump-adviser-jenna-ellis-twitter

Was it all just a big misteak?

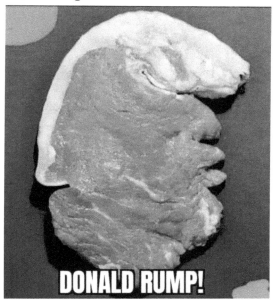

The World's Most Expensive Sheep

… Baa None!! Unbaaaaalieveable!! (see (‿|‿) X3).

As kids (sorry, they're goats) flock back to school, this week saw the sale of the most expensive sheep ever (in Scotland). With the cash, an offspring bought a really expensive car and drove around in it in swimsuits. It was a lamb bikini. 😂

https://www.insider.com/worlds-most-expensive-sheep-sold-scotland-490000-2020-8

Caption Competition

Let me know your 'wording' for the caption by **noon on Saturday 12th September**. There is a prize for the best entry.

♫ Stevie's Puuuuuzzles
(and Last Week's Answers)
of the Week ♫

► What's the difference between a train and a teacher?
There are probably a few possible answers.
Let me know yours.
A pint for the best/or the one I receive.

Last Week's Answers
► France – the first French fry was not cooked in France … but where?
In Greece!!!!! Sorry about that.
► Exam - I'm livid that I failed to remember how to write 1, 1000, 51, 6, and 500 as Roman numerals in my exam. How come?
I, M, LI, VI, D Roman Numeral numbers for those listed.
► Snooker – highest break in snooker? Easy, medium and very 'Tricky' answers on this one!! A drink on me if you get all three!! I think I probably owe a couple of pints here, as someone came up with a solution that wasn't exactly mine but worked.

► Answers 147, 155 (with a free ball and extra red/black) (‿|‿) X4

162 – Pretty unlikely, but it but would involve either somebody having a 155-point handicap/start, doing the 155 option (above) and then potting the re-spotted black straight off the break.

A similar option, would be if somebody did 155 worth of fouls and then did the 155 option, with a free ball and then potted re-spotted black.

Next Week's TV

» Yorkshire Ripper Documentary BBC4 9 pm Tuesday 1st Sept

» Terminator 2 Judgement Day. The first time of Arnie's 'I'll be back' return as T2. ITV 9 pm Thursday 3rd

(‿|‿) **X1** Al Gore Rhythm!!!!

(‿|‿) **X2** If not aware, a simple card game where the person left with the Ace Loses.

(‿|‿) **X3** Unbelievable Jeff … Mutton/Mutt and Jeff

https://en.wikipedia.org/wiki/Mutt_and_Jeff

(‿|‿) **X4** Jamie Cope in 2006 and Alex Higgins reported to have scored a 155 break. Nobody ever has done a 162 as it is only theoretically possible for the purpose of this quiz.

Issue No 22

SUNDAY 13TH SEPTEMBER 2020

Joy of Six!!!

Headlines:

- ▶ Tory rebellion widens over Boris Johnson's bill to override Brexit deal
- ▶ Coronavirus: 86% of doctors in England expect second wave within six months

Leeds Utd Update - Liverpool 4-3 Leeds

Hi All …

Football Returns with Leeds in the Top Flight Again … Hurrahhhh!!!!

Football is back, including Leeds with a fantastic, albeit 'pointless' performance at the Champions, Liverpool. Surely, it must give us confidence. I'm not sure if anyone saw this elsewhere, but there's not such a good display of footballing skill below. Miss of the Century!!

https://talksport.com/football/758723/watch-worst-miss-of-all-time-fails/

Feedback from the Last Issue

I'm going to start off with some more feedback this week and incorporate my brother's 'Health and Safety

Moment' at the same time –

- ► My bruv replied and said he was 'shaking his head' that much at the 'gags' of the last edition that he had a sore neck. 😂
- ► Rosco replied (wow!!) with a … 'I think you're losing the plot, mate'!!! (Gotta have found it first, of course!!!) But just to get a reply from Ross is enough for me. Yes, I might be getting a bit of Cabin Fever, BUT we all know, however, what the first sign of Madness is … It's Suggs coming up your drive!!!!!! So, I'm okay atm. 😂

Feedback

- ► Once again, I'll reciprocate all feedback received by saying thanks to all those who told me the definition of the word 'zillion' … it means a lot. 😂 I've got lots of these. I can see a pattern developing!!!!!!

In this Week's Issue –

- ► Joy of Six – New Rules - The Good Six Guide?!
- ► Contracting CV
- ► Britannia Rules the Waves and Waives the Rules!!!! Last Night of the Prom and Contract negotiations
- ► Bonkers Boris
- ► Caption Competition
- ► Stevie's Puzzle(s) of the Week
- ► Next Week

Joy of Six!! Not for the Seven Dwarves or the Magnificent 7, of course?!

As the new 'Rule of 6' lockdown measures come into force from Monday, we all try to follow the safe six/good six rules. Only six people can meet in and outdoors.

So, in a forest far, far, away … one of the seven dwarves isn't happy. Well, six of them aren't Happy!! But one of them is Grumpy (or going to be). I know, six of them aren't Grumpy, but one will be grumpier!!! And, what if they do get CV and become tired and start sneezing, etc., etc? And if Snow White is still living with them (or is she with The Prince?), then two will be Grumpy, and two won't be Happy. Thank God Doc is there for CV and Mental Health issues. 😄 At least they don't have to read this!!!

And what about the Magnificent 7? I think we get the drift, Steve!!!

Contracting CV

But cases ARE up, and we do have to be careful. I met up with my old school buddy last week who works in the building trade for a few socially distanced beers. He mentioned he was having to be very cautious atm about contracting CV, especially when working at other people's houses (sic). Anyway, he went ahead, and now CV works for him. 😄

That reminds me, I'm applying for another job atm,

and I've nearly finished filling in my CV ... 😄

Britain Rules the Waves or Waives the Rules?!

Ironically, as Last Night of the Proms 'blasted' out Rule Britannia this week (controversially for some), instead of Ruling the Waves, BJ was waiving the rules regarding the Withdrawal Agreement. I certainly can't take credit for this headline/gag, BUT you do know my views on plagiarism - see Issue No. 7.

Strange also that in the week we signed a no tariff trade deal with Japan - The UK-Japan Comprehensive Economic Partnership Agreement - was agreed in 'Principle', we do this (waive) on a previously agreed document. So, if a fully signed declaration can be changed, I'm not sure what chance the Japan deal has or, of course, any other agreement now or in the future covered by the Rule of Law. All very strange!!!

Bonkers Boris

Whilst many commentators are still unsure of BJ's intentions regarding the reneging, altering or, call it what you will, there is, of course, always the Sanity Clause to rely on.

Sanity clause ... https://www.youtube.com/watch?v=U7RhAMTB1Qs. 🤭

Classic Marx Bros. If I've used this before, I am sure you will agree it is worthy of duplication as it still stands the test of time ... but, again, you do know my view on plagiarism.

Speaking of duplicates (copying), one part of this sketch referenced a joke about duplicates, that I never quite 'got.' However, now (40 years on from the first time I saw it), the power of search engines and understanding the timing of the joke (nearly 100 years ago) has helped to clarify – see (‿|‿) **X1** if interested!!!

Caption Competition 👣

The Winner ... *Sprinting Back from Scotland and getting nowhere fast, it's the return of the Lockdown Mess Monster looking to burger it up again!!!* 🍔

Thanks for all your responses. There are two winners this week - Mr Tony B and Nic Magoo, but only one can be printed!!! A prize/pint to both.

🎵 Stevie's Puuuuuzzles
(and Last Week's Answers)
of the Week 🎵 👥

▶ Q. I weigh nothing, but you can still see me. If you put me in a bucket, I make the bucket lighter. What am I?

Last Week's Answers –

▶ What is the difference between a train and a teacher?
One goes Choo Choo, and the other says spit it out (i.e. don't chew chew).

Next Week's TV

» Strangers on a Train, 3.25 pm, Thursday 17th, TCM
» The Miracle of Morgan's Creek, 1.05 pm, Film 4

All t' best, and stay safe,

Steve

(⌣|⌣) **X1** Duplicates –

Groucho: Don't you know what duplicates are? - Chico: Sure. **Those five kids up in Canada.**

This is a pun (*jeu de mot*) based on the confusion of the terms for multiple siblings born at the same time with the word 'duplic**ates**.' It only becomes clear when spoken because the endings are pronounced alike: 2= twins, 3 = tripl**ets**, 4 = quadrupl**ets**, 5= quintupl**ets**, 6 = sextupl**ets**

In particular, Chico would have been thinking of Dionne quintuplets, born in Canada in 1934, "the first quintuplets known to survive their infancy." For a long time they were the subject of much public interest and many news stories.

Issue No 23

Tuesday 29th September 2020

New Measures Imposed

Headlines:

► COVID-19 tests that give results in minutes to be rolled out across world

Leeds Utd Update - Sheff Utd 0-1 Leeds

Hi - CCC - attached as usual when you see … 😄

Hold your horses!!! SFTWS is here!!!

Apologies for the delay, but I've taken a couple of days off. I was once sacked from my calendar-making job for that. 😄 Bad news for you as it's given me extra time to come up with even more crap jokes!!!

Serious Bit to Start - and SFTWS Continues by Popular Demand

To be serious for once. As very confusing new measures (even for the PM and Gillian Keegan MP to comprehend, to name but two) sweep across the country, we need to be careful and continue to watch out for each other. The new measures are not as severe as before (or a full lockdown), but they could be even more damaging given they are compounding on everything that has gone before. Given all of this, it seems appropriate for SFTWS to continue AND it does so by popular demand (‿|‿) **X4.**

All Okay?

Or should I say, 'How are you in yourself?' Whatever that means!!??? A greeting for contortionists, perhaps!! That reminds me (No, it doesn't, Steve!!), I once attended a contortionist competition at Butlins a few years ago. I entered myself ... and won. 😄

In this Week's Issue –
- ► Football. Always Kick Off with Footie - When Leeds Win, of Course!!
- ► Toilet Rolls and Panic buying
- ► French Open Tennis
- ► Student Chaos
- ► The Return of Trump – Like a bad smell!!
- ► Quiz, etc
- ► NEW FEATURE – Under the RADAR (Random Alerts Detailing Alternative Reports)
- ► Next week

Football ... and the Hand Ball Rule

Another Leeds Utd win!!!!! A tight, tense game (with much talk and innuendo about Leeds' new centre-back, Koch!!!), and we scraped a 1-0 win.

There was another charity raffle in the pub as usual before the game. A woman was offering a 'pound a strip.' (sic). Most of us paid her £2 not to!! The prize, would you believe, was a toilet ... so it was a win/loo situation. 😄

The hand ball rule is now causing much debate and confusion, and VAR is hardly helping. Everyone is 'up in arms' … but that means they will probably be penalised for hands in an 'unnatural position.' 😄 Or perhaps they could say they are only breaking the rules in a 'specific and limited way' as BJ said with the Brexit Agreement!!

Also this week, the Oxford Utd Team bus wouldn't start due to an alcohol-based Covid spray. It's mad, and you just couldn't make it up (see below for more details). It's just insanitiser!!!!

https://www.oxfordmail.co.uk/sport/18750934.covid-alcohol-spray-grinds-oxford-uniteds-team-bus-halt/

Toiler Rolls and Panic Buying

Speaking of loos, I'll not make all the toilet rolls jokes as, like the shops, I'm all out of them and using old newspapers again. The Times are rough. 😄

A report on the news this morning said that a record £80m was spent on toilet rolls in March. Mass bulk buying has started again after recent Lockdown announcements. Many shops were also reporting shortages in piñata, paella and sombreros at the supermarket. I thought to myself … Hispanic buying. 😄

To my Hispanic friends who have not been buying in

a silly fashion, I've been saying to them, "Muchos." It means a lot to them. 😂 The pattern continues in a new language!!

Due to loo roll shortages, thieves have been stealing them from a local cop shop … and, would you believe, they have taken the toilets as well. Police say they are looking non-stop for the culprits, but they 'have nothing to go on.' 😂 (‿|‿) X1.

French Open Tennis

I'm just watching the French Open Tennis as I draft this, so I decided to look up on Google who hit the first ball at last year's event. My computer said … 'Server could not be found.' 😂

I met my wife in the middle of a tennis court. **You work that one out (‿|‿) X2.** 👫

Next week, I'll be googling 'medieval male servant.' (‿|‿) **X3. You should be able to work that one as well!!** 👫

Students – More Chaos.

The situation at uni is now as bad as it was in schools … to a degree. 😂

Thousands are in lockdown – many are 'scared and confused.' Some are putting up quite amusing messages in their windows, though.

See https://www.bbc.co.uk/news/newsbeat-54323132.

I do have sympathy for them and the ensuing chaos. It

was reported last night that many were experiencing a problem as they weren't allowed to use shared laundry rooms. I'm not sure this was a real issue, really, given it was unlikely any of the 'Great Unwashed' would use them this year!!! To be fair, many students do start their laundry but never finish. Halfway through - they always throw in the towel. 😄

My wife and I had a long argument last night as to whose turn it was to do different aspects of the laundry. So, as usual, we played poker to decide. Eventually, I folded. 😄

The situation with students seems to have calmed down a bit today, and they should be ok to come home for Xmas. The whole Student Debating Society were actually going to rebel against the new lockdown measures, but they were talked out of it. 😄

Trump Returns to SFTWS

As the candidates go head to head in tonight's TV debate, it seemed apt to bring him back for this issue.

» Supreme Court Appointment
  Trump controversially nominates Amy Coney Barrett for the Supreme Court. Many years ago, I became involved in the American Courts. Whilst on holiday, a guy said to me 'Have a nice day,' and, when I didn't, I sued him. 😄
  Trump Pays Just $750 in Income Tax. This

story of Trump is hanging around like a bad smell.

Trump's defence is that he has converted to atheism as it's a non-prophet organisation😂. In addition, he claims all his business products were flatbreads with a picture of Mohammed on them - as all naan-prophets are tax exempt (best said with the American drawl accent). 😂

» Cheesy Trump
On another Tax related matter, Trump is introducing a 30% tax on shredded cheese. This is part of his plan and slogan to **Make America Grate Again.** 😂 More cheesy cheese puns next week.

Tax vs Fine

Don't forget. A fine is a tax for doing something wrong. A tax is a fine for doing something right.

🎵 Stevie's Puuuuuzzles
(and Last Week's Answers)
of the Week 🎵📻

► Therein Lies the Conundrum – what word in English contains 10 separate words without rearranging any of the letters? What is the Word???

See (⌣|⌣) **X5** for a clue.

Last Week's Answers –

▶ I weigh nothing, but you can still see me. If you put me in a bucket, I make the bucket lighter. What am I?

A hole.

Under the RADAR (Random Alert Detailing Alternative Reports)

Stories you may have missed?

▶ Flying medics in the Lakes … https://www.bbc.co.uk/news/uk-england-54331994

▶ Flushed Down the Toilet. A worthy story, given a hot topic in this edition. https://waterbriefing.org/home/water-issues/item/17631-bbc-report-reveals-dual-flush-toilet-systems-waste-billions-of-litres-of-water-every-week

▶ Ask Attenborough. Kids quiz the National Treasure … https://www.bbc.co.uk/news/video_and_audio/headlines/54333080/sir-david-attenborough-gets-quizzed-by-kids-after-plea-to-world-leaders-to-save-nature

Next Week –

» Spitting Image Returns. Ruder than Ever!!!! Britbox Streaming from 3rd October

» A Life on our Planet – Streaming on Netflix

» The Searchers 4.05 BBC2 Sunday 4th. Classic

Western with Big Leggy!!!

All t' best, and stay safe.

Steve

(‿|‿) **X1** I couldn't resist one of my oldest and favourite and, of course, crap jokes!

(‿|‿) **X2** A net/Annette!

(‿|‿) **X3** 'Page could not be found'!!

(‿|‿) **X4** Everyone was asked. One person said yes. A clear majority!!!!!

(‿|‿) **X5** Clue – it's only a 7-letter word.

Issue No 24

Monday 12th October 2020

Tiers for Everyone!!

Headlines:

► Covid: UK at 'critical juncture' as No 10 unveils three-tier alert system

Leeds Utd Update - Leeds 1-1
Man City, 3rd Oct

🍪 CCC – Comic Cone Chortle. Attached for your amusement!!!!!!

Hi All

New Lockdown Measures

Going to press, Boris has been outlining new Lockdown restrictions today, but all I can say atm is that nobody is content, and everyone is in Tiers. 🍪 Liverpool will be *the* only area in a Very High Tier 3 so far.

In other related news, it looks like I'll be quitting my part-time job at the cat shelter – as they have reduced meowers. 🍪

Always Kick Off with Football – even when there is no Premier League!!!

No proper football this weekend. I'm still drying out from the walk back after last week's Leeds v Man City

1-1 draw. BUT what a game!! Followed by some bizarre results.

Liverpool fans were loving the Man U result for 24 hours until they were hammered by Villa. Liverpool were also fined £10k under CV (rule of 6) for letting 7 in. 😆 (⌣|⌣) **X1.**

At normal football time, 3 pm this Saturday, I was actually watching Countdown (sic) – with Richard 'Twice Nightly' Whiteley and Carol 'Vord the Board' Vorderman. See Stevie's Puzzles below.

It was the last one in the series. So, it must have been the Final Countdown. 😆 (⌣|⌣) **X2.**

Pay-Per-View Controversy

In their wisdom, the Premier League decided to charge nearly £15 a time for some games. Surely, it's not a good or right time?! We'll just have to go back to listening on the radio or reading about it int' newspapers – a much cheaper version of 'Paper View.' 😆

Gunnasaurus is Extinct – Arsenal pay £45m for a player and £150k a week, but they sack the team mascot … see Under the RADAR!!!

In this Week's Issue (isn't that enough already, Steve?) –

- ▶ Traffic Lights – Further Lockdown and Last Chance Saloon
- ▶ Health and Safety Moment and the Whining

Dog
- ▶ Wind Power – Blowing in the Wind for once!!
- ▶ EU Deal Hope. The Great British Break Off!!
- ▶ Vice President Debate – Pence: Fly in the Face (on Head) and Fly by (not on) Seat of His Pants!!!
- ▶ Brother Andy/Andrew and Charity Event/Walk. Watch this Space
- ▶ Stevie's Puzzles of the Week. Stevie Does Countdown
- ▶ Parachuting Gran
- ▶ Under the RADAR (Random Alert Detailing Alternative Reports)
- ▶ Feedback and Contributions
- ▶ Next Week

Track and Trace

The Govt revises the current £12 billion T&T system and resorts to basics by giving everyone a pencil and a thin sheet of paper. 😊 (⌣|⌣) x3.

New lockdown measures are set to be announced involving some kind of traffic light system. But nobody knows what or where. This is unfolding as we go to press, so I'm sure it will be covered in much more detail in the next edition.

Potentially Last Chance Saloon and Health and Safety Moment – The Whining Dog (a True Story)

Saturday might now prove to be the last chance for a while to go to the pub (with others), given today's announcement. As we know, masks are essential against CV, but they can also be a danger - especially to waitresses and table service. I'm not sure whether it's because of spectacles steaming up or because they can't see their feet properly.

Anyway, on Saturday, a waitress tipped a full tray of Pinot Grigio all over a dog on the floor. The soaked dog subsequently shook himself dry and covered everyone close with vino. So be careful when wearing masks and remember the w(h)ining dog story. Very funny, I thought, but perhaps you needed to be there?! 😂

For a bit of personal development, please also see another whining dog story that many may have already seen and benefited from (‿|‿) **X4.**

High-Tech Traffic Lights System and Green Means you can Go (to the loo)!!!

Again, another true story from Saturday Night's Last Chance Saloon. There was a very 'high-tech' traffic light system in the pub on the door to the gents. It involved two cards – one side red and the other green - to indicate how many were in the toilet. Anyway, it fascinated us for hours (sad, I know). When I did finally go, I forgot to turn over the cards, but at least I used the one-way cistern and, unlike the fly on Vice President Pence, the one on the urinal finally got peed off!! 😂

Wind Power

It has hardly been a breeze for Boris on CV, but as we await news on new restrictions, all he gave us last week at the Virtual Party Conference was hot air. He is apparently a huge fan of Wind Turbines. He suggested *every house would have some wind power* by 2030 and would be spending £500m on this policy (experts suggested it would cost 100x that amount). All of this would need lots and lots of tiny fans … and yet all was opened up with very little fan fair. 😂

A friend of mine (No, he isn't, Steve) was killed after being caught up in an airplane turbine. In many ways, he will be mist. 😂

EU Close to a Deal … The Great British Brake Off!!

Let's continue the theme of things in our waters (like the offshore fans). News this week (overshadowed by other events) suggested that there is now a 66% chance of a deal on Brexit as there has been some movement on fishing. My understanding is that if it's fish in our waters, we want 'em. If it's people, you can have 'em. 😂

Vice President (VP) Debate – and Fly in the Face of Popular Opinion (well, Mike Pence)

Speaking of wind, you could say that I Trumped a little prematurely in the last edition … given everything that has happened since.

As mentioned above, there was a fly in the ointment in the VP debate last week. The most interesting thing that happened was a VP fly past and sit in/on Mike Pence's head for over two minutes. A fly sat on his face and as one commentator said, 'Politics returned to normal – boring and not answering the question.'

Love him or hate him; this is something you can never say about Trump!!

🎵 Stevie's Puuuuuzzles
(and Last Week's Answers)
of the Week 🎵 👥

- ▶ Countdown – (Genuine) 'Numbers Rounds' from the popular show. This was the first one I saw (S51 Episode 2) and you should be okay with this. To do it properly, give yourself 30 seconds. Spookily, one is double the other. Was it fixed??!!
  - » 25, 6, 5, 7, 10, 9 … 420
  - » 100, 10, 8, 8, 10, 4 … 840
- ▶ What made it stranger was one of the contestants, who had a PhD in Mathematics (sic), couldn't get the first one and ended up saying he'd got 419. See if you can work out how he managed to do that???!!! It's much harder than getting the right answer.

- ▶ Finally, a trickier one from S51 episode 3
  - » 50, 75, 6, 3, 10, 4 … 888

Last Week's Answers –
- ▶ Therein Lies The Conundrum – what word in English contains 10 separate words without rearranging any of its letters? What is the word???
  The word is **THEREIN … the words are 'the, there, he, in, rein, her, here, ere, herein, and of course Therein!!!!**

Andy/Andrew RIP [10 Year Anniversary]

This week on Thursday (15th Oct), it will be ten years since my brother Andy/Andrew tragically passed away (wow, where did that time go!!!??). A charity event/walk was planned like the one on the first anniversary, but Covid, of course, has delayed our plans. Watch this space, though. As most of you knew him, please raise a glass at least on Thursday. Hopefully, I'll still be allowed to go to the Grove Pub this week to do so, but I might be sitting outside.

Sky Diving Gran

Speaking of chaaaaaarity, hopefully, you saw this. A 90-year-old Gran jumps for charity in a once-in-a-lifetime experience – see below.

https://theprestonhub.co.uk/2020/10/04/90-year-old-granny-takes-on-15000ft-skydive-for-local-childrens-hospice/

I think a parachute jump is the scariest thing that I have ever, ever, ever … refused to do.

I DID do a parachute jump once. You are attached to an instructor, and you jump out of the plane together. So, in the plane, they attached me to this bloke, and we jumped out. It was really frightening because halfway down, he said to me, "How long have you been an instructor?" 😄

After that, I had a parachute for sale. 'Used once, never opened. No strings attached.' 😄

See (‿|‿) X5 for Trump in crashing aeroplane shocker!!!

Under the RADAR (Random Alert Detailing Alternative Reports).

Stories you may have missed …

Hottest September on Record

It was hardly barbecue weather here but, around the world, fires have been raging. I did manage one barbecue recently and invited Harry Corbett, Sooty and Russell Crowe. I **bet** you cannot guess what they had. The former had a sweepstake and the latter a small and lightly grilled lady (perhaps it was Barbie) in a bap. Anyway, RC was Gladiator. 😄

https://www.bbc.co.uk/news/science-environment-54442782#:~:text=September%20was%20the%20

warmest%20on,record%20high%20for%20the%20 month.

Underground Marathon World Mental Health Day 'Beneath The Surface' …

Sally Orange, from Stafford, said, "We have called this marathon 'Beneath the Surface' because, like mental health, you can't see what is going on in someone else's mind."

https://www.yorkpress.co.uk/news/18770510. deepest-underground-marathon-bid-charity/

Gunnasaurus – In football news, Arsenal pay £45m and £150k a week for a player but sack the mascot as the furlough scheme ends … unbelievable, Jeff!!

https://metro.co.uk/2020/10/11/paul-merson-says-some-of-thomas-parteys-arsenal-wages-should-have-gone-to-gunnersaurus-13403985/

Cage Fighting – To be shown on BBC. The budgie didn't stand a chance. 😔

https://www.telegraph.co.uk/mma/2020/10/06/ exclusive-bbc-broadcast-live-coverage-mma-event-first-time/

Mars – Will be closest to earth over the next few days than it has been in 25 years.

https://www.forbes.com/sites/ startswithabang/2020/10/05/watch-mars-make-its-closest-approach-to-earth-until-2035/#167441ae7a44

Pub Desks – I've already got mine in the Grove (pub) but can't have any visitors - unless you live with me!!!!
https://www.bbc.co.uk/news/uk-54472414

Feedback and Contributions

All welcome. The plan was to have a ghost/mystery writer for one of the sections – but the contribution failed to show by the deadline!!!!!!!!!!!

Next Week's TV

> » The Bridge C4 Sunday or Catch Up. Not the same as The Bridge, the Norwegian/Danish Cop drama, which is also well worth a look.
> » Shaun of the Dead, 11.10 pm, ITV4, Thursday 15th October.

Stay safe and take care,

Steve

(‿|‿) **X1** I know you may have heard it a few times, but given the weird world of football atm, I thought it was worth another attempt.

(‿|‿) **X2** Saved you further gags, the show that breaks all records, and it's the last one in the series … The Vinyl Countdown.

(‿|‿) **X3** Track and Tracing Paper. Do you recall the old-fashioned toilet paper (when I was at primary school, anyway) that was like tracing paper? It was like Tigger - couldn't deal with Pooh!!!

(‿|‿) **X4** https://personalexcellence.co/blog/howling-dog-story/

(‿ | ‿) **X5** Trump in Aeroplane shocker …

Four people are on a crashing plane, but there are only three parachutes.

The first person to grab a parachute is Brad Pitt, and as he reaches for the door, he says, "My family and my fans need me; surely you will understand." Off he goes.

The next person to grab one is Donald Trump. "I'm the most intelligent president this nation ever saw; I will do great things to this country," he says, and he jumps out.

Left in the plane are an old man and a young school boy. "Go on, take the last one," the old man said. "I lived a long and fulfilled life." Hearing that, the schoolboy answered calmly, "Don't worry; we'll both be okay. Our most intelligent President yet just took my backpack."

Issue No 25

Trick or Treat or is it Track and Trace?

Headlines:

► No 10 under growing pressure to U-turn over free school meals

Leeds Utd Update – Aston Villa 0-3 Leeds, 23rd Oct

Hi,

CCC – attached as usual for your amusement and pleasure when you see the 😄 sign. As requested by some, there is a new fixed(ish) time for the email - Monday at 7 pm!!!!!!!!!!!!

Thanks for your constant feedback and emails (see below). I am always happy for anything anyone wants to throw my way. I can't guarantee I will respond, but if it's decent, I will promise to nick it as you know my view on plagiarism😄. The rule is 'topical' but funny is, of course, optional!!! See Write (Wrong) of Reply below – 'New Feature'. Please look out as well for the Audience Participation (AP) symbol. 👥

The clocks went back this weekend; I'm not losing any sleep over it, though. 😄

I was once fired from my job at a clock factory (We don't believe you, Steve), and after all the extra hours

309

I put in. 😄 In Covid terms, it feels like clocks have gone back to March!!

In this Issue –

- ▶ Football – Bam Bam Bamford
- ▶ Trick or Treat
- ▶ Tiers of a Clown – Manchester 3 Leeds 2. For once happy with this result!!
- ▶ School Din Dins
- ▶ Silent Trump – A Quiet Week?!
  - » New Law - Only Trump Supporters Can Vote?!
- ▶ Trade Deal Japan – is it Fantasy (Island) Next?
- ▶ Feedback - Write (or Wrong) of Reply? 👥
- ▶ Stevie's Puuuuuzzles (and Last Week's Answers) of the Week
- ▶ (⌣|⌣)(⌣|⌣)(⌣|⌣)

Hat-Trick Bamford

🎵 Do, Do, Do, Do … Patrick Bamford!!! 🎵

I always kick off with football BUT I was genuinely going to avoid it this edition until Leeds' demolition of previously undefeated Villa. Leeds climbed temporarily to third in the 'Table.' Headline writers have been hoping for this to happen for years, but it's only Patrick's 2nd ever hat-trick. Ironically, his only other one was against Leeds.

Shame he couldn't have scored one more as then Villa's efforts would really have been … four nothing.

Trick and Treat, or is it Track and Trace?

With Halloween approaching, it's the other T&T which continues to be the horror show. If you get a knock on the door this week, who will it be?! Perhaps we could get the kids to do T&T while they are out doing T&T!!! Surely, they can't do any worse! Can they do the annual Trick and Treat online?!

I'm not even sure kids are allowed/advised to go out this year, are they? It certainly would seem strange. When my kids were young and we went out with them, I would always dress up as a demon and the wife as a ghoul. Everyone knows demons are a ghoul's best friend. 😬

(Track and Trace) T&T and Perhaps Isolate?

TnT... not Dynamite, of course, as solutions shouldn't be blowing up all the time!!

Anyway, a Govt official has drawn up new plans without a rough draft to go on. Unfortunately, this has now disappeared without a trace. 😬

Reports today suggest that the isolation period may be cut from 14 days to 7 or 10. NOT because it's working, but because people aren't adhering to it. Is that the right way round!!?? Perhaps, the opposite of isolate needs to be yousoearly. I might need to work on that one X😬X. I'll add this to my 'Blooper' list –

New Feature, coming soon. Bet you can't wait?!

Tiers of a Clown – when there's no fun around!! Perhaps the Covid-Kokie can help - see (‿|‿) **X3.**

The new Govt approach looks like it is all going to 'end in Tiers' as more people go into more severe forms of lockdown. This week, Manchester finally went into Tier 3 over a (relatively) paltry £5m sum. The Govt then announced a support package of billions which may have assuaged the mayor, colleagues and residents if it had been announced earlier.

I'm not sure whether all this is a lack of communication or deliberately antagonistic, but it is all very strange. There were calls of a North/South rift, given this new support was announced as London entered Tier 2. **Do you think there is a North/South divide?** Is it like the one that exists/existed in America, General Lee speaking?

Manchester Pubs Close (and now many more as other areas move into Tier 3) - if not offering a 'substantial' meal. Whatever that means!!!!

Given the above, my mate from over the Pennines came over to Leeds for a beer. Due to our Tier 2 measures, however, he decided to dress up in drag and pretend to be my wife, which allowed us to sit together inside. Anyway, it was obvious to all (when they did the checks) that he had a Wigan address.

He's gone home now to look for a new job (as he is

currently out of work coz of the pandemic). The next time I saw him, he was on the corner of the street, and the back of his anorak was leaping up and down. People were randomly chucking money at him. He told me, 'This is my livelihood, now.' 😂 Better than busking, I suppose??!!! Remember, steal a man's wallet, and he'll be poor for a day. But teach him to play an instrument, and he'll be poor for the rest of his life!!!

CV is bringing communities and rivals together. One of my neighbours is a Man U fan, and we are having a water fight later - as soon as the kettle boils. 😂

Anyway, many politicians are asking for a credible exit plan or strategy or, at least, an exit sign, but as we know, they are ALL on their way out. 😂

See also Under the RADAR and 'Manchester Workaround' below.

Latest: There could be (more) Tiers before bedtime as the Govt are currently considering a Tier 4!! https://metro.co.uk/2020/10/25/fresh-plans-being-made-for-stricter-tier-4-restrictions-13477467/

School Din Dins

Speaking of Manchester, difficult as it is for me to say as a Leeds fan, but you have to be impressed by Manchester United's Marcus Rashford and his fight for school dinners for the needy. Many, now including Leeds Utd players, have stepped up to the 'plate' to join this cause. There are much 'wider' issues here, but keeping with the footy theme, I can only see this as another Govt own goal!!!

I always made a note of exactly what was on my lunch plate at school. Just in case I had to describe it later when on a drip in A&E, I would then know exactly what to say. 😄

'Substantial' could never be used to describe school meals, but it is the word of the moment. Pubs in T3 are allowed to stay open if they provide a substantial meal, but what does that mean? Thanks for all the feedback I've received on the definition of the word 'substantial' … it means a lot. 😄

A Silent Trump!!

This week's presidential debate passed without much hoo-hah. It was more civil and the only thing to report was Trump saying in the same sentence that he 'takes full responsibility for CV,' but it wasn't his fault … it was Chiiiina!!!!

Only Trump Supporters Can Vote?

In other election news, Trump is thinking of bringing a new law in, where only people who support the incumbent can vote … everyone else is forBiden. 😄

Anglo-Japanese - Trade Deal

Following Brexit day, on 31st January 2020, the UK has been free to strike its own deals for buying and selling goods and services around the world. The UK has finally signed the first one 'in principle' (only) this week ... with Japan.

https://news.sky.com/story/brexit-uk-and-japan-to-sign-15-2bn-free-trade-agreement-in-tokyo-12111609

All these trade wars are tariffying!!! But perhaps the next appropriate one will have to be with Mr Roarke and Tattoo on Fantasy Island. https://en.wikipedia.org/wiki/Fantasy_Island

Are you old enough to remember this? Perhaps this one is only for the 'oldies' who may recall the TV series.

The best trade I ever made was when I got a car for the wife - what a swap that was!!! To be fair, only an old-fashioned, banged-up model ... but the car was in good nick😄. On a related matter, I saw a sign yesterday that said ... 'Watch for Children.' Again, I couldn't turn that down. I got a pocket watch and a wristwatch as a swap for my twins. 😄

Can We Trump Trump?!

I don't like to build up Trump's tactics, but perhaps sometimes he's spot on. He said, as part of his Roadmap and trade war with China ... 'It's my way, my way or the Huawei!!'

Back to the EU Withdrawal, my prediction (well, it's always been the same, really) is it's like trading a sausage for a seabird. The deal has taken a tern for the wurst. 😄

Write (or Wrong) of Reply - Any better suggestions?
👥 Come on, do some of the 'Heavy Lifting'!!

As the German composer's nanny would say ... "Feedbach time." 😄

It might be straight to 'Bloopers', that one! Well, I could hardly use my ... 'still not had any feedback from my chicken pellet business,' again, could I? Oops, I just did!!!

In Response to Last Edition's Issue – (Genuine!!) Feedback from Lena

Dear Steve,

I write with regard to your latest newsletter and specifically the anecdote about the barmaid with the steamed-up glasses spilling wine over the dog. It wasn't Pinot; it was Sauvignon. As a more pedantic point, I'd like to point out that I was there, and the joke about the w(h)ining dog isn't funny. And I've tried. The story is funny. The whining dog joke is unnecessary and not funny.

Yours sincerely,

Mrs Lena Backwell

SFTWS – Thanks, Lena. I must have missed you (unlike the wine) in the pub, but thanks for this. As mentioned earlier, topical is preferably; funny is optional and NOT mandatory!!!

🎵 Stevie's Puuuuuzzles
(and Last Week's Answers)
of the Week 🎵👣

Question no 1 - What do the four people below have in common … ?

► Pele – famously advertised Viagra and now promoting a new version that goes straight in the eye. It doesn't do much but makes you look hard. 😑 To celebrate his birthday, he has got a new single out (sic) about a football curse. Perhaps linked to Viagra? https://www. fourfourtwo.com/news/pele-releases-single-to- mark-his-80th-birthday 'Listen to the Old Man'!!

► Cliff Richard – I really want to do something for him to celebrate his 80th birthday, but I can't think of a song to use. 😑

► Sir Geoffrey Boycott – closing in on another century, perhaps!!

► Asad 'Booyah' Abdulahi – Somalia Pirate. Quite relevant, given the Isle of White Piracy incident this weekend https://www.bbc.co.uk/news/uk- england-hampshire-54684440

► Question No 2 – Linked to Henry VIII and Ann Boleyn below. Where do you go when you get your (a) head and (b) hand chopped off? **See (‿|‿) X1.** Very 'old' (I first heard this when

I was 6!!!) but I couldn't resist. Like I said, topical!!!

▶ Question No 3 is on the themes of 'exits' above. **Enter through one, exit through three. Once you succeed, I am on thee. What am I?**

All answers will be in the next edition.

Last Week's answers

Well, if you had a try, I'm sure you worked them out!!!!!!

Under the RADAR (Random Alert Detailing Alternative Reports). Stories you may have missed …

▶ President … Whatsisname, erm, Doo-dah, of Poland - Gets Coronavirus … https://www.bbc.co.uk/news/world-europe-54672736

▶ Six Horseman of the Apocalypse!!!! See the image at the end of this issue. Chris Whitty and Sir Patrick Vallance join the four famous horsemen!!!! Thanks to 'Burkey' and Private Eye for this contribution.

▶ Chilling account of how Henry VIII planned Anne Boleyn's beheading https://www.theguardian.com/uk-news/2020/oct/25/chilling-find-shows-how-henry-viii-planned-every-detail-of-boleyn-beheading and, perhaps, her brother Ten Pin 🎳 (⌣|⌣) X1 He certainly knocked them off/over!!

▶ You may have heard this Report Headline on

BBC Sport as 'Clever Dick a Moaner as he gives away a penalty for Kilmarnock.' https://www.bbc.co.uk/sport/football/54580486

► Manchester Workarounds - cooked up to avoid Tier 3, perhaps? - https://www.thetimes.co.uk/article/manchester-bars-cook-up-schemes-to-dodge-tier-3-ksc55dp60

Next Week's TV –

» A Beautiful Mind – Film 4, 6.20 pm Tuesday 27th October

» IT – ITV2, Friday 30th at 9 pm

See ya' soon. Stay safe, and take care …

Steve

(͜ | ͜) **X1** Ten Pin (Boleyn).

(͜ | ͜) **X2** Covid-Kokie

You put your household in
Your children out
Eat out, Help out,
Spread it all about

You do the Covid-Okie
And U-turn around
What the hell is
this all about?

Oh, the Covid-Kokie
What a Covid-Jokie
Oh, the Covid-Kokie
Masks on
Spaced out

Ra, Ra, Ra

Issue No 26

Vaccines Announced with 90% Efficacy

Headlines:

- ► GPs in England will scale back care to deliver Covid vaccines
- ► Trump's vote fraud claims go viral on social media despite curbs

Leeds Utd Update - Crystal Palace 4-1 Leeds, 7th Nov

Hi all … CCC is attached for your pleasure when you see this sign. 😋

Sorry for the delay, but I have genuinely been for a CV test. Hopefully, it's just precautionary.

Knock, knock.

Who's there?

Dishes.

Dishes who?

Dishes the ghost of Sean Connery. 😋

Yes, the legendary Bond actor passed away at the age of 90 (not from Covid, but he has been 'shelf-isolating' for some time). Sean is a regular in SFTWS see (◡|◡) **X1** from Issue No. 8 (true story).

Sad News.

Since the last edition, when I mentioned four famous people becoming octogenarians (see below), coincidentally, four actors/comedians (inc. Sean) have sadly passed away:

► Sean Connery, Bobby Ball, Geoffrey Palmer and John Session.

In addition, many of you may have heard that Simon Metcalfe, the first ever HA/HE Jefferson City goalkeeper sadly passed away recently. A truly great bloke. He (and all) will be sadly missed.

A Shot in the Arm for the Nation?

At going to press, news is announced about a potential vaccine with over 90% efficacy levels - more in the next issue. CV may be hoping for a second wave of Trump. 😂

Any vaccine might be restricted to the elderly first, which is a shame as kids shoot up so quickly these days. 😂

PIN Pub Shocker

No football this week, especially after Saturday's Leeds result. A related (true) story.

As some know, I've been going to the pub to watch some games. On a couple of occasions, I couldn't remember my PIN. It's weird as I normally have a good memory, but I had to contact my bank and unlock it. A week later, it happened again.

When I went to the pub last Monday for the Leeds v Leicester game, the same thing happened for the 3ʳᵈ time. So, once again, I had to use my other card/pay cash.

This time, however, when it came the time to pay, the waitress said, 'Do you mind coming to the bar? The digits 3 and 8 don't work on the mobile keypad and haven't for some time!!!'

I had my mask on by this time but I think the waitress could see the astonishment in my eyes!!! Not only has this happened twice before, so why didn't you tell me then? But also, now you know 2 of the digits in my PIN. I might be in touch for a reminder if it happens again!!!

NB - Have you ever tried walking up to someone whilst they're at a cash machine wielding binoculars and saying ... 'Sorry, was that a 5 or a 6?'

(‿|‿) X1 On a related matter of memory, I once found a genie's lamp, and I rubbed it. A genie popped out and granted me either a good memory or a very long penis/thingamyjig (genie speak).

I forget now what I asked for. 😄

New Lockdown 2 - the Sequel (It's never going to be as good as the original – especially if the vaccine mentioned above is as effective as suggested).

Anyway, here we go again!!!! It really does feel like

déjà vu. Did I already do my déjà-vu joke??

To make things easier (for both of us!!), perhaps I could just go back to March and rerun the entire SFTWS from Issue No 1. Many will say, 'What's the difference??'

The issues have dramatically 'evolved' over the last six months and are now a little longer, as you know (based on feedback, of course)!!!!

NB. Speaking of feedback, not much this week as my electric guitar amp has fused, and there is no word this week from Mrs Lena Backwell either. 😄 Well, I could hardly use my Chicken Pellet business 'line' again, could I? Ooops!!

New Feature: How Are You Coping and What Ya Been Doing?

Let me know. 👀

It's not supposed to be rhetorical. **How are you doing and what is helping through lockdown?**

- ▶ No 1. JP/Poc's Bar - The Drunken Bastard – that's the name of his bar, not JP's nickname. He's been called much worse!!

A 'mate' of mine has built his own bar in his garage during lockdown **(see photo in (◡|◡) X2).**

Unfortunately, he suffered from termites during construction, and many of them turned up and asked, 'Is your bar tender here?' 😂

Last night, $f(x)$ and a sarnie walked into his bar, but he had to say, 'I don't serve food or cater for functions.' 😄

It is quite a surreal place, however, as you can experience the past, present and future at his bar - it's always tense. 😄

Finally, Van Gogh turned up last week, and he was let in. I arrived and asked VG if he wanted a beer. He replied, 'I have one ear.' 😄

- ► See more 'bar and pub' shenanigans below in the quiz!!!

Next Week – No 2 (Basket Weaving) and No 3 (Turn Your Life into a Musical). **Unless you come up with summat else!!!!** 😄

TRUMP – 'You're Fired'

The Disunited States of America.

After the protracted vote, lawsuits continue. Does Trump finally accept his fate, and has he packed his bags? Maybe he has lost his case. 😄

Only China and lawyers are the winners. The latter should be buried 20 feet under as deep down they are nice guys, apparently. 😄

Love him or hate him, watch 'Trump: Tweets from the Whitehouse' (on Catch Up). It's quite incredible!!

A Silent Trump (a phrase worthy of another 'outing', surely)!!

As Trumpelstiltskin is told to put his 'Big Boy pants' on, nobody could have predicted this saga unless you had 20/20 vision. 😄

Women should be worried as there is talk (given the success this time) that the next one will be an all-mail election. 😄

At going to press, there was still no concession, and this one could run and run. One of Trump's Republican Senators, and a Judge to boot, won his election despite not having any thumbs. 'Justice Fingers' ran unopposed. 😄

No Normal Bonfire Night but there are still Fireworks

Bonfire Night was not the traditional night as expected this weekend, but at least many experienced fireworks at home.

America is not alone, however, as one particular guy fawkes it up over here as well!!! Unfortunately, the vaccine won't come soon enough for some.

There were some arrests, though. A policeman arrested two kids. One for drinking battery acid, the other for eating fireworks. They charged one and let the other off. 😄

Even though I couldn't attend my neighbour's party this year, I still sent round some bangers and rocket for them to enjoy. My sausage and lettuce sarnies didn't go down well, as I think the kids were expecting fireworks. 😄

Under the RADAR (Random Alert Detailing Alternative Reports)

Stories you may have missed …

- ▶ Boris is at it again … he wrote two tweets to the next US President, depending on the outcome https://www.bbc.co.uk/news/uk-politics-54892098

- ▶ Golf https://www.bbc.co.uk/sport/av/golf/54897477
  Is this the best golf shot ever?! And he was only wearing one sock, and/or he had to change his trousers after – u can work it out!!!!!!!! https://edition.cnn.com/2020/11/10/golf/jon-rahm-hole-in-one-masters-spt-intl/index.html#:~:text=Jon%20Rahm%2C%20on%20his%2026th,ahead%20of%20the%20

- ▶ Double Trouble - Melania Trump. Blames it on someone else as uses a 'Body Double.' I wonder when and where Mrs T. switches. https://www.dnaindia.com/world/report-fake-melania-trends-after-new-photo-reignites-wild-melania-trump-body-double-rumours-2852576

- ▶ Rocky 4 – A Director's Cut. Sly chops the robot. It's strange that he thought this was pivotal/needed in the first place!! https://screenrant.

com/rocky-4-directors-cut-sylvester-stallone-drago-video/

🎵 Stevie's Puuuuuzzles
(and Last Week's Answers)
of the Week 🎵👥

Bar Quiz – Keeping with the JP Bar theme –

► Comic Sans, Helvetica, and Times New Roman walk into a bar.
"Get out!" shouts the barman. WHY?

► An amnesiac walks into a bar. He goes up to a beautiful blonde, and what does he say?

► A weasel walks into a bar. The bartender says, "Wow, I've never served a weasel before. What can I get you?" What does the weasel ask for?

Last Week's Answers

Question no 1 - What do the four people below have in common?

► Pele – famously advertised Viagra and is now promoting a new version that goes straight in the eye … It doesn't do much, but it makes you look hard😂. To celebrate his birthday, he has got a new single out (sic) about a football curse. Perhaps linked to Viagra? https://www.fourfourtwo.com/news/pele-releases-single-to-mark-his-80th-birthday 'Listen to the Old Man'!!

- Cliff Richard … I really want to do something to celebrate his 80th birthday, but can't think of a song to use.
- Sir Geoffrey Boycott – closing in on another century, perhaps!!
- Asad 'Booyah' Abdulahi – Somalia Pirate. Quite relevant, given the Isle of White Piracy incident this weekend https://www.bbc.co.uk/news/uk-england-hampshire-54684440

Quiz Answer 1. All could have said 'Aye Matey' (I am eighty) this month. Regarding the pirate, it is irrelevant how old he is, BUT I picked one who is closest at 76. See the following link.

https://en.wikipedia.org/wiki/List_of_pirates#Piracy_from_the_20th%E2%80%9321st_century:_1901%E2%80%93

- Question No 2 – Linked to Henry VIII and Ann Boleyn below. Where do you go when you get your (a) head and (b) hand chopped off? See. Very 'old' (I first heard this when I was 6), but I couldn't resist. Like I said, topical!!!

Quiz Answer 2. Head Office and a Second-Hand Shop!!!!

- Question No 3 - On the themes of 'exits … Enter through one, exit through three. Once you succeed, I am on thee. What am I?

Quiz Answer 3. A t-shirt!!!

Next Week's TV

- ▶ Jojo Rabbit - Sky Premiere Friday at 8 pm
- ▶ Blade Runner 2049 – Thursday, ITV 4, 9 pm

'See ya' soon … Stay Safe and take care …

Steve

(‿|‿) X1

♫ Stevie's Faaaaact of the Weeeeeek!! ♫

Sean Connery was banned by the car company for doing **Citroen** ads because of his accent/pronunciation (work it out!!!).

(‿|‿) X2

Issue No 27

Monday 30th November 2020

Bully Patel

Headlines:

- NHS to enlist 'sensible' celebrities to persuade people to take coronavirus vaccine
- UK universities fine students £170,000 for Covid rule breaches

Leeds Utd Update - Everton 0-1 Leeds, 28th Nov

Hi all … CCC is attached for your pleasure when you see this sign. 😅

I think I missed a week. I must have felt sorry for you.

Further to last edition, my test was negative, btw. Thanks for all your concern!!!!

It's Advent Time Again!!!!

I hope you have your advent calendars ready for tomorrow. I'm not sure they will be available next year. Their days are numbered. 😅

Last year, I had a Microsoft one, but after three or four days, I couldn't open any more of the windows.

I used to make Advent Calendars, but I was fired for taking two days off. So, I then nicked a normal calendar on my way out – and got 12 months. 😅 (‿|‿) **X1.**

In this Week's Issue –

▶ Tiers of Despair/This Pair (BJ and Rishi). No more Tier/Tear 'puns,' I promise!!)

▶ Bully Patel

▶ Trump – The Non-Concession Concession

▶ Diego and Darth Vader

▶ Quiz – Back to the future

▶ Lena Feedback

Tiers of Despair/This Pair

Another bizarre week as the PM announces the 'coming out' of lockdown this week ... and into, ermmmm, lockdown!! Rishi also announces new plans for the economy.

Most have come out in a worse tier than when they went in. So, what was the point? In addition, why have five days 'off' at Xmas if it's just going to mean a longer lockdown? As always, as we know, there is no F in strategy. 😆

Priti Patel - You Can't Beat a Bit o' Bully(ing)!!

Priti Bully

The Home Office Sec of State, Priti (Vacant) Patel, is accused of bullying, but the prime minister stands by his 'man' again, even though she breaks the Minister's Code. Is there anything ministers can do that will get them sacked/make them resign? Is there another Dom Cum saga looming?

I witnessed lots of bullying at school, but I was ok as my best mate was John Someoneyourownsize … and, for some reason, they picked on him. 😄

Funnily enough, I'm still giving some of the school bullies my dinner money to this day … every time I go to McDonald's. 😄

But our school had the most average bullies in the country … they were all so mean. 😄

More Lost to Covid, Including Celebs

It's been another week where we lost many more to Covid and a couple of 'legends' in their own and very different right:

- ► Darth Vader (the body, NOT the voice). Aka David Prowse, who was also the Green Cross Code Man for those old enough to remember. Why did Darth Vader cross the Road? I've just told you - because he was the GXC Man and was helping kids across. OR to get to the Dark Side!!! You decide. 😄
- ► Diego Maradona – arguably the best footballer who ever lived and another man with two sides

to his character. Watch 'Diego Maradona,' the documentary if you get the chance, which is streaming atm. My view has certainly changed since the 'Hand of God' moment in 1986. Whether that is because I watched the above or just through the passage of time, I don't know. I suspect it's because Leeds are currently being managed by an Argentinian (◡|◡) X2.

https://www.news18.com/news/football/know-the-truth-behind-video-of-an-overweight-diego-maradona-2654487.html

Coronation Street celebrates 60 years

https://www.manchestereveningnews.co.uk/news/tv/coronation-street-unveils-first-look-19364700

Trump – the Non-Concession Concession

Speaking of bullies, Trump continues to linger, is impossible to get rid of and continues to kick up a real stink, AND he's been silent but deadly (on CV). Sounds like a Trump to me. 😂 He is, personally, still predicting himself to win 51 States – including the State of Denial. 😂

I'm a Celebrity Get Me Out of Here

Due to CV, this year is held in a Welsh Castle and a better celebrity list than usual given in the UK. I only really watch it for Ant and Dec, and the (eating) trials, and some of those are becoming boring. If you 'tape' it, you can watch an hour in about 15 mins!!!

Look out for the spin of the series in the new year. It's about religious insects who go climbing. It's called, 'I'm a Celibate Flea, Get My Mountain Gear.' 😄

Victoria Derbyshire, who is in it this year said, (sic), before she came in, she went to the doctors as she felt like a supermarket. The doctor asked how long she had felt like this … 'Ever since I was Lidl,' she replied. 😄 She was obviously telling a 'joke' of sorts, and it does seem to fit in perfectly, here with all in a similar vane.

Lena is Back - Feedback

Dear Steve,

I know Radio 2's Popmaster is popular with your readers who are, so-called, "working" from home. Well, I have discovered that if you listen to the show on a digital radio and on your Highways England laptops at the same time, the digital radio signal is received several seconds before the BBC Sounds version. So, there's no more '1 year out' for clever-clogs Lena! I'm easily able to beat the contestants and get 3 outta 10 every single time!!!

Mind you, it's getting a bit boring now. So, I usually end up switching over to the dreary and depressing drivel that is inevitably to be found over on Radio 4 nowadays. And before you start sticking up for Jane Garvey, I'm talking about those unfunny PC comedy shows - not Woman's Hour! Tuning into yet another worthy Radio 4 play about the Holocaust or slavery is far preferable to listening to Ken Bruce playing Billy Ocean's latest LP and hearing Belinda Carlisle's 'Heaven Is a Place on Earth' for the 25th time that week.

Best get some work done and put my bra on before my line manager video calls me - the pervert.

Yours sincerely,

Lena Backwell (Mrs)

♫ Stevie's Puuuuuzzles
(or Quiz & Last Week's Answers)
of the Week ♫

Film Quiz = Alternative Film Titles. **Name the film.**

I had some feedback that the quizzes have dried up a little recently, so I thought I'd go back to the future (and I don't mean Michael Fox in the garden centre again).

1. Courageous Organ
2. This Mush Is All Made Up
3. A Blustery Departure
4. He's Happy He Ate the Woman
5. Sharp Jogger
6. Roman Assignment
7. Cowardly Jog
8. Pastoral Fantasies
9. Righteous, Sinister and Repulsive

10. Let William Go

Answers will be in the next edition. Next week, just in time for Xmas, I'll do an alcohol quiz. I won't be getting any in the pub unless I go to Harrogate on Xmas Day (still in T2). I hope that's okay, Mick M and Dave R!!!!

Last Week's Answers

- ▶ Comic Sans, Helvetica, and Times New Roman walk into a bar.
  "Get out!" shouts the barman. WHY?
  "We don't want your type in here."
- ▶ An amnesiac walks into a bar. He goes up to a beautiful blonde, and what does he say?
  "Do I come here often?"
- ▶ A weasel walks into a bar. The bartender says, "Wow, I've never served a weasel before. What can I get you?" What does the weasel ask for?
  "Pop," goes the weasel!!

Under the RADAR (Random Alert Detailing Alternative Reports)

Stories you may have missed …

- ▶ None this week, back next!!!!!

Next Week's TV

- ▶ Blade Runner 2049 – Sky

'See ya' soon. Stay safe and take care …

Steve

(‿|‿) **X1** I know I might have used some of these before, but just like falling off the bike, I am happy to recycle!!!!

(‿|‿) **X2** Peter Mayhew, the actor who played Chewbacca, died exactly 19 months ago (sic). He was eaten by cannibals and appeared in the 'A bit chewy' section of the paper. 😂

https://www.google.com/search?q=when+did+chew bacca+actor+died&rlz=1C1GCEO_enGB876GB876&oq =when+did+chewbacca+&aqs=chrome.1.0l2j69i57j0l4 j0i22i30l3

(‿|‿) **X3** Leeds Manager Marcelo Bielsa https:// en.wikipedia.org/wiki/Marcelo_Bielsa

Issue No 28

Thursday 24th December 2020

Brexit Deal for Xmas?!

Headlines:

► English regions should go into Covid Tier 4 now, scientists say

Leeds Utd Update - Man Utd 6-2 Leeds, 20th Dec

Hi, everyone - CCC – attached as usual for your amusement and pleasure when you see the 😆 sign.

All t' Best for Crimbo!!!!!!!

A Merry Xmas to all my 'avid' 'friends' and 'readers'!!!

I do see a bright future for you, but no present. 😆 (‿|‿) X1

Anyway, as we close in on a Fishy Brexit Deal and our first Xmas Dinner without Brussels 😆 …

In this issue –

► Would You Adam and Eve it??
► There is no Santa!! Or is he from Gdansk?
► Ready for Xmas?
► A Year to Forget but Full of Crackers
► Nightmare Before Xmas
► Lorry/Dover Pile Up
► Trump – Budget and Border Chaos

- ▶ Stevie's Puuuuuzzles – Last Week's Answers
- ▶ (⌣|⌣)(⌣|⌣)(⌣|⌣)

Would You Adam and Eve it??

Yes, a Merry Xmas to all. Or should I say what Adam said to the first woman on Earth on this day many years ago … "It's Xmas Eve Eve, Eve." 😂 (⌣|⌣) **X2**

Apologies for the delay, but I was waiting for the Tier review. That announcement was then overshadowed by new Tier 4 restrictions, and after that by the travel ban and the lorry pile up and the cancellation of Xmas and then the Brexit Deal, then the new Govt initiative … 'Eat Sprouts to Help Flout.' 😂

There Is No Santa!! Or Is He from Gdansk?

Don't tell the kids … but there is no Santa Claus!

If he did exist …

Tradition has it that the modern character of Santa Claus was surrounding the historical Saint Nicholas (a 4th-century Greek Bishop and giver of Myra). Others say he is from around Gdansk and speaks North Polish 😊 as that's where his workshop is!!! His workshop is closed atm as many of his workers have had to elf-isolate.

I had to do one of these gags at least!! As long as you've got your elf ... oops!!! 😊

Or maybe he is from Horsforth, Leeds?!!!!

Ready for Xmas?

Anyway, are you ready? 😊 I finally got my Xmas tree yesterday. The guy selling it to me said, 'Are you going to put it up yourself? 'No, in the corner of the room,' I replied. 😊

A Year to Forget but Full of Crackers

Covid has made this year one to forget, but it's going to be a tricky Xmas Edition, given that after nine months of telling Xmas Cracker jokes ... what do I do now?

But my concerns are small alongside those of the Queen. What the heck is she going to say this year? The only thing I can tell you for certain this year is that her speech has been renamed 'The One Show.' 😂

Speaking of crackers, I've got my Xmas cheese and crackers (or Cheeses of Nazareth, as I like to call them) ready for Xmas Eve. However, it won't be the same without a trip to the pub and a belly full of hand-pumped real ale. There was no Zoom at the inn, anyway. 😂

In Germany, tradition is for sausage with cheese on Xmas Eve ... but, perhaps, they are just panic buying coz of the Brexit/Covid situation. In other words, planning for the wurst käse scenario. 😂 (⌣|⌣) **X3**

Nightmare Before Xmas

As lorries pile up and there is complete chaos at Dover. One lorry, carrying snooker equipment, jack-knifed and left cues for miles. 😂 Unfortunately, there were a few collisions as well.

> ► A lorry carrying an assortment of wigs collided with a Vicks Vapour Rub lorry. Police are still combing the area, but there is optimism that there will be no congestion by morning.

- A cement truck crashed into a minibus transporting prisoners to jail, who subsequently escaped. Police say they are looking for dozens of hardened criminals.
- And, of course, the lorry load of terrapins smashed into a van full of tortoises. Police said it was a turtle disaster. 😄

Trump in Budget and Border Chaos

More on borders. With about a month to go before President-Elect Biden's inauguration, our good friend Mr T is aiming to go out on a real high (low?). He has amazingly vetoed Covid relief aid and the approval of defence budgets. Given this was set up by his own staff/party, it does seem to 'border' on stupidity … just like Canada and Mexico, I suppose😄. Speaking of Mexico and borders, with the wall still not built, Trump now takes Xanax for his anxiety. Well, Hispanic attacks, anyway 😄😄. There's a double-up in there!!!

Anyway, with his last few days in the White House, I bet he will be having one or two parties over Xmas and the NY. I'm sure he'll put on a super spread. 😄

'Tis the Season for Men with Long White Beards

It's a great time of year for men with white (grey) beards, and as many know, I've been cultivating mine – see below.

Pai Mei Pay Stevie P

Pre Mini Quiz - Do you know who doesn't have a beard but does dress in red and gives to the children? 🐾 (⌣|⌣) X4

🎵 **Stevie's Puuuuuzzles -
Last Week's Answers** 🎵🐾

Alternative Film Titles
- ▶ 1. Courageous Organ – Braveheart
- ▶ 2. This Mush Is All Made Up – Pulp Fiction
- ▶ 3. A Blustery Departure – Gone With the Wind
- ▶ 4. He's Happy He Ate the Woman – Gladiator (Glad he ate her)
- ▶ 5. Sharp Jogger – Blade Runner
- ▶ 6. Roman Assignment – The Italian Job
- ▶ 7. Cowardly Jog – Chicken Run

- ▶ 8. Pastoral Fantasies – Field of Dreams
- ▶ 9. Righteous, Sinister and Repulsive – The Good, The Bad and The Ugly
- ▶ 10. Let William Go – Free Willy

Under the RADAR (Random Alert Detailing Alternative Reports).

Stories you may have missed …

- ▶ Deputy Dawg. Puppy escapes alligator attack and now works with the police.
  https://www.bbc.co.uk/news/av/world-us-canada-55325370
- ▶ Isle of Wight Shocker. There will be Tiers before Bedtime (I think I said I'd not use any of these again!!)
  https://onthewight.com/tier-3-isle-of-wight-jumps-up-from-tier-1/
- ▶ Death of Darth Vader (AKA David Prowse). In case you missed it, the full report is in last issue.
  https://www.bbc.co.uk/news/entertainment-arts-55117704.
  Every year, he comes round mine to 'feel my presents.' But not this year. I won't repeat my Chewy joke from the last issue.
- ▶ Last person to put two feet on Everest recently. The official height of Mount Everest is reviewed and revised. https://www.npr.org/2020/12/08/944152693/everest-gets-a-

growth-spurt-as-china-nepal-revise-official-elevation-upward?t=1608673810963

▶ Battle of the Planets (Not the vintage kids TV show). Planet Alignment https://edition.cnn.com/2020/12/21/world/christmas-star-jupiter-saturn-solstice-scn-trnd/index.html

Next Week's TV

» Some Like it Hot on BBC2, Xmas Day

» Trainspotting C4 11 pm Mon 28th

» Groundhog Day/Home Alone (1, 2 & 3) would seem very apt this year – on various channels. I didn't realise the latter was a futuristic film when it came out initially. 😂

'See ya' soon … Stay safe and take care.

Once again, Merry Xmas and Happy NY (if I'm not back before then). We really will have to flatten the curve, then. 😂

Byeeeeeeeeeeeeeeeeeeeeeeeeeeeeeeeeeeee!!!

Steve

(‿|‿) **X1** Not good, I know, but keeping with tradition of crap jokes. A crap joke is NOT just for every week (after the development of Covid) but for Xmas as well!!

(‿|‿) **X2** or just 'Eve, Eve as might be the 24th before the edition is issued. said 'Aye Matey' (I am Eighty) this month.

(‿|‿) **X3** Wurst and käse are German for sausage and cheese.

(‿|‿) **X4** Marcus Rashford

Issue No 29

Monday 25th Jan 2021

Vaccine Hope – Variant Hell!!!

Headlines:

► Ministers won't commit to reopening schools in England after Easter holidays

Leeds Utd Update - Leeds 0-1 Brighton, 16th Jan

Hi everyone - Happy New Tier!

- CCC attached as usual for your amusement and pleasure when you see the 😄 sign - I bet you've missed me/it?!

Apologies for the delay but, good news for you, I developed a bad case of writer's bl- 😄

In this Issue –

► Covid Nightmare Continues
► Happy Birthday, Steve. Ten months of lockdown, so keep helping others and yourself!!!
► America – A Bastion of Democracy???
► Capitol, Let Us Ransack Your Democracy!!! Always start with Capitol Let Us!!! Too contrived? 👥
► End of an Error - Trump Goes Phbbbt (But Will

He Be Let Off) – And Will a Whiff Remain?

- ▶ Weather Armageddon. Snow and Floods - Plagues of Egypt
- ▶ Police Records and No Records
- ▶ Stevie's Puuuuuzzles (and Last Week's Answers) of the Week 🏚️
- ▶ Under the RADAR (Random Alert Detailing Alternative Reports)
- ▶ Next Week – TV, etc. and Mrs Lena Backwell – She's Back after her Covid issues!!!!!
- ▶ (‿|‿)(‿|‿)(‿|‿)

Covid Nightmare Continues

Lockdown continues. Some hope, perhaps, in vaccine?

The new variant (to be named Covid Mc Covid Face 😂) is more contagious but, apparently, also more lethal.

A Help With Covid?

I went to the chemist and asked the assistant what helps with Coronavirus. She said, 'ammonia cleaner.' I said, 'Sorry, I thought you worked here.' 😂

She did say, however, that her boyfriend worked at Leeds market, and he could get me a vaccine for 3 quid … or 2 for a Pfizer. 😂

What's the Difference Between 2020 and 2021?

There are a few things to consider about 2020, but 2021 looks like most, if not all, will be the same:

  1. The dumbest thing I ever bought was a 2020

planner.

2. Normally, stay away from negative people. 2020: Stay away from positive people.

3. The world has turned upside down. Old folks are sneaking out of the house. and their kids are yelling at them to stay indoors!

4. This morning, I saw a neighbour talking to her cat. It was obvious she thought her cat understood her. I came back to my house and told my dog ... We had a good laugh.

5. Every few days, try your jeans on just to make sure they fit. Pyjamas or 'trackie' bottoms will have you believe all is well in the kingdom.

6. Does anyone know if we can take showers yet, or should we just keep washing our hands?

7. I never thought the comment, "I wouldn't touch him/her with a 6-foot pole," would become a national policy, but here we are!

8. I need to practice social distancing ... from the refrigerator.

9. I hope the weather is good tomorrow for my trip out to the bins!

10. Never in a million years could I have imagined I would go into a bank with a mask on and ask for money. 😁

Happy Birthday Steve

It was my birthday this weekend. I'm cough, cough and five-sixths of a year old!! Given, as you know, that lockdown started on my last full birthday, that means we've now been at this for ten months and there's still no end in sight. Although the vaccine does give us a boost/shot in the arm!!! No wonder we are all struggling a bit. **Keep going, keep in touch with me and others and keep helping and/or asking for support if needed.**

America – A Bastion of Democracy – An End of an Error!!!

Remember it should be that in a democracy, every vote counts ... whereas in feudalism, every Count votes. 😂

Lots of issues across the pond since the last issue. There are close to 500,000 CV deaths now, but the aftermath of the election probably tops it. It's tricky to know where to begin, but ... 'Grammar' would always say you should start with ... capital letters ...

Capitol, Let Us Ransack Your Democracy

Chaos ruled as an angry mob stormed the Capitol Building and inner sanctum of American democracy. Trump becomes the only president to be impeached twice. We still don't know where this will go.

End of an Error!!!! Trump Goes Phbbbt (But Will He Be Let Off?) Will A Slight Whiff Remain? 😂

Trump leaves and goes off silently and deadlier than ever could have been expected. Perhaps it was because of this quietness that in the last few days in the White House, everyone is going around saying Pardon Me? Rudi Giuliani certainly has a bad case of wind as he's saying it over and over again. 😄 See more about Rudi G in Under the RADAR below as well!!!

I heard that, pardon!!!!! One for the oldies, perhaps... https://www.youtube.com/watch?v=MfWr9JNUWfg

See also https://www.youtube.com/watch?v=37Apscp3hsM

This coincidentally talks about the FA Cup and Sheffield Wednesday, which is on TV as I write this – spooky!!!!!!!!!!!! (‿|‿) **X2.**

Trump Leaves White House and is Barred from Entering!!

Anyway, as Biden is inaugurated, Trump won't be allowed back in as the White House is now forBiden. 😄 Yes, I did it before, but now it's the other way 'round!!!

With all the issues, it was, however, a good day for diversity as Kamala Harris became the first lady of South Asian descent. Interestingly, there is now the first Second Gentlemen in the White House (sic).

Biden has made numerous executive orders already (repealing many of Trump's policies. Which, in turn, repealed many of Obama's). Anyway, one of them is to reintroduce blocks of cheese across the whole of the USA ... he really does want to make America grate again. 😄

Weather Armageddon – Snow, Rain Floods

NB – If it rains cats and dogs, you might step in a poodle!!! 'Icy what you did there.' 😄

The situation recently in America is snow joke, but neither is the weather atm. Perhaps the storms are no worse than usual, but with Covid, it does feel like the (ten) Plagues of Egypt (‿|‿) **X1** are upon us. First the snow, then the floods and now more snow. Anyway, 'snow days' aren't really the same if you don't have anywhere to go or are not allowed to go in the first place!!!!!

Stevie's Snowman/Snake?

I made a snowman the other day. Well, more like a snow snake (see photo at the end of this issue). I was going to go back and put some arms on it, but five minutes after this photo was taken, he (or should be 'she' and you know why – **answers on a postcard, please** 👫) collapsed and disappeared.

Perhaps she snuck off to my vegetable patch to pick her nose. 😄 All this just goes to show that time waits for snowman (‿|‿) **X3.**

Snow Travel (at All)

I had to finally get the car out after two days and couldn't find my ice scraper (it had probably melted 😄). So, I used my credit card instead and managed to get 20% off. 😂

Q - How does the man who drives the snow plough get to work?

The other day, I was nearly knocked over by a big lorry laying salt when he came too close to the pavement and splattered me all over. I did shout after him, though. Through gritted teeth.

Floods – I'll pick this up properly in next issue (I think you have had enough for one edition), BUT at least the Mancunian who won the speedboat on Bullseye (in 1981) can finally use it. See also Under the RADAR for the Bullseye killer.

There are still more answers for the Govt to answer ... but I'm not sure they give a dam.

Police Records

Priti (irresponsible Patel) is also under pressure from all sides for misplacing her Sting music collection (sorry, I couldn't resist ... Police Records). Alan Partridge did it better and the other way round ... https://partridge. cloud/scene/?id=evdnKOtILtCu

Criminal records have gone missing, though, and this could have a serious impact on many investigations.

Certainly, there are a few Police records (sorry, songs) that spring to mind that might be quite apt atm because of Covid:

- ▶ Don't Stand So Close To Me, So Lonely, Voices in my Head, Hole in my Life, Walking in your

footsteps and, sadly, I Can't Stand Losing You.
And, of course, when it does finally get to us all,
De do do do de da da da or Radio Gaga (oops,
Queen) as well. 'That's enough, almost apt
Police songs, Steve.' Sorry, my brother was a
big fan of the Police when I was growing up, so
I can recall many!!!

On a serious note, mental health will need to be
addressed for many years to come.

🎵 Stevie's Puuuuuzzles
(and last Week's Answers)
of the Week 🎵📻

Keeping it easier this edition ... to help you back in
slowly.

- ► What can you never answer yes to?
- ► What gets bigger the more you take away?
- ► What always ends everything?
- ► I shave every day (obviously, not me!!!). Who
  am I?
- ► Don't forget the ones elsewhere about the
  snowplough and the Mrs Snowman (above)!!
- ► Final Quiz Question below in Under the RADAR
  about 'Fish.'

Some might have more than one answer and/or come
up with your own!!!

Under the RADAR (Random Alert Detailing Alternative Reports)

Stories you may have missed …

- ▶ Rudi G – https://www.nytimes.com/2021/01/22/ us/giuliani-concedes-that-an-associate-did-ask- for-20000-a-day-to-help-trump-post-election. html
- ▶ Barbados – https://barbadoswelcomestamp.bb/
- ▶ Rees Mogg – our fish are happier now they are British fish? https://www.youtube.com/ watch?v=eiKmqY_RNME – even though they can't get into British Markets?!
- ▶ Quiz Question. Can you name three fish beginning and ending with the letter K? (◡|◡) X4.
- ▶ Bullseye Killer – https://www.birminghammail. co.uk/news/midlands-news/cop-who-nailed-the- bullseye-19630446
- ▶ Frank Lampard Sacked – https://www. skysports.com/football/news/11668/12198327/ frank-lampard-sacked-by-chelsea-after-18- months-thomas-tuchel-set-to-take-over There's more to follow on this, I'm sure!!!!

Next Week's TV

- » Netflix – The Queens Gambit (more on 'Chess' next week, perhaps)
- » Blues Brothers ITV4 Tuesday 26th January 9 pm

» Mad Max 2 – ITV4 10 pm
» Sky Films – various - King of Staten Island. Different but watchable.

'See ya' soon … Stay safe and take care.

Steve

(‿|‿) **X1** https://en.wikipedia.org/wiki/Plagues_of_Egypt

(‿|‿) **X2** I was asked many years ago, 'Can you tell me your availability to run a football team in Sheffield?' I said, 'I can't manage Wednesday.' 😊

(‿|‿) **X3** Just one of my throw-away lines but would you believe there is a film? - https://www.imdb.com/title/tt0136566/

(‿|‿) **X4** Killer Shark, Kilmarnock (a plaice in Scotland) and King-Sized Haddock. 😊

Issue No 30
Monday 22nd February 2021

Roadmap Outta Lockdown

Headlines:
- ▶ Covid: Boris Johnson unveils lockdown exit plan: schools and social contact first
- ▶ COVID-19 lockdown easing in England: key dates and phases in the roadmap

Leeds Utd Update - 19th and
23rd Feb – Wolves 1-0 Leeds and
Leeds 3-0 Southampton

Hi All - CCC is attached as usual for your amusement and pleasure when you see the 😄 sign.

No Football

I'm not kicking off with football this week as Leeds avoided (in the end) a Valentine's Day Massacre but still lost v Arsenal and then were unlucky but still lost again v Wolves.

Roadmap Outta Lockdown for my Birthday or Easter??

BJ is announcing measures as we speak. More in the next issue. Anyway, keep the end of March/Easter free for 'Tinnies' (at least) outside the Grove (pub)!!!

'I'll be back' as I said to the landlord - **Pubs back open by Easter (ish)** - Just in time to use my fave Arnie joke (‿|‿) **X1**). I'll have to check, but I suspect I will have used it this time last year!!!!

Or, perhaps, even a new one along the lines of he could play the 'Vaccinator' in a new film with a new catchphrase … 'You'll be Back.' 😂

In this Issue –

- ▶ Vaccines
- ▶ Zoom
- ▶ Captain/Major Tom and David Bowie
- ▶ Beware Drug Farmers
- ▶ Uber Court Challenge – U Berated by Judge!!!
- ▶ It's Snow Joke for Texas – JR Ewing - Must be Turning in his Grave
- ▶ Trump - No Drama Anymore
- ▶ It's a Sin – It's a S in (a pub)!!!!
- ▶ Stevie's Puuuuuzzles (and Last Week's Answers) of the Week
- ▶ TV – Missed to Catch Up and Next Week.
- ▶ (‿|‿) (‿|‿)(‿|‿)

Vaccines

A major part of why we might be back to 'normal' soon is the continuing success of vaccines. There is talk about doing them all night, but this might just be a shot in the dark. 😂

I have a mate who is helping with vaccines atm and ensuring that everyone keeps their distance in the queue. I've always said you really do know where you stand with him. 😄

Zoom

As the working week literally zooms by, we reach another weekend. Many of you, I know, use these jokes/material for weekly 'ice breakers' on Zoom meetings. Shame they're not remotely funny. 😄

I was on a Zoom Team Meeting this week with my colleagues - see below.

It just happens that our (A) Team is very cosmopolitan and all colleagues are actually from different countries. When I enquired, "Can you see me?" they responded ...

"Yes."
"Oui."
"Sí."
"Ja!!!!!!!" 😄

Here are another couple of Zoom clips you might have seen since the last issue, but they're worth another look.

▶   Parish Council Meeting

https://www.youtube.com/watch?v=l17UIwAFOyk

► Pussy Cat in Court

https://www.theguardian.com/commentisfree/2021/
feb/11/lawyer-cat-funny-texas-rod-ponton-judge

Given it's on Zoom, I suspect it will be settled 'out of court.' 😂

Finally, because people are beginning to hate Zoom calls, I'm getting a lot of perks from colleagues to shut them down. I suppose you could say I'm making ends meet by making meets end. 😂 (⌣|⌣) **X2.**

Farewell to (Honorary) Major Tom Moore and David Bowie Link

Farewell to Major/Captain Tom, who sadly passed away since the last edition. What a remarkable man. It seems appropriate that he gave so much to the fight against the pandemic and (now) shares his name with the drug-induced space song lyric. Also, Ashes to Ashes ('That's enuff Captain Tom/Bowie links, Steve').

NB – Beware: Drug Farmers out there!!

Speaking of drugs. With the recent cold weather, beware that the police might not be too far away, checking out those lofty drug farms ... Neighbours in the Netherlands can anonymously report their suspicions if they see a snow-free roof, indicating a heated cannabis farm.

https://www.independent.co.uk/news/world/europe/

melting-snow-being-used-police-find-cannabis-farms-netherlands-10036057.html

Uber Court Challenge – U Berated by Us!!!

I suspect Sir Tom didn't take many taxis with all his walking, but the judge didn't just ask the taxi-driving normal questions. As Peter Kay would say, "What time do you start? Been busy? What time do you finish?"

The judge rules in favour of the drivers. So, the boot is on the other pedal this week as a judge told Uber where to go!! 😄 (⌣|⌣) X3

As a footnote, my mate is called Spartacus, and when he orders a taxi, someone else always seems to end up with it as everyone claims it. 😄 'Taxi for Mr Parker, please!!! (⌣|⌣) X4

It's Snow Joke for Texas – JR Ewing (Remember Him?) Must Be Turning in His Grave!! (⌣|⌣) X5

The world is a crazy place atm, BUT surely nothing can be weirder than Texas running out of oil and freezing over. Yes, JR and Bobby's Lone Star State, where Texaco comes from (hence the logo).

As a National Emergency is declared in Texas, Senator Cruz is under 'fire' as he jets off on holiday (see below) whilst everyone else freezes and starves.

https://www.independent.co.uk/news/world/americas/us-politics/ted-cruz-cancun-united-airlines-texas-b1805739.html

Will they be able to find diesel or petrol for cooking and heating in the next few weeks? Well, your gas is as good as mine. 😂

Called the Lone Star state, perhaps, as Beyonce is the only star to come from there 😂 (‿|‿) **X6.**

Speaking of another Route 66 (not Joe below), it was partly frozen/covered on one side as Arkansas refused to clear the side on the Texas boundary …

https://nypost.com/2021/02/18/arkansas-leaves-texas-side-of-shared-road-covered-in-snow/

Trump – No Drama this Edition

I'm not going to blame the above on Trump … yet!!!! But there has been some TV worth watching (and not just for Trump bashing). The amazement goes both ways but is worth a watch. Truly astounding –

- ▶ The Trump Show
- ▶ Trump takes on the World

Anyway, they probably didn't impeach Trump because he is orange already. 😂

Trump the Movie Star

But as he did actually appear in a number of films (Home Alone 2, Wall Street), he has now resigned from various actor unions. Before he was made to, I suspect!!!

https://www.dailymail.co.uk/news/article-9225083/Donald-Trump-RESIGNS-Screen-Actors-Guild-rant-filled-letter.html

Impeachment (or perhaps I'm Peach/I'm Orange, is what he should say) is something he's earned and a stain on his legacy, whereas Clinton had the legacy on his stain. 😏

IT'S a SIN

A TV series set during a previous and terrible pandemic. The only difference was that pubs remained open!!

Somebody pointed out that my doppelganger was in it. **What do you think???** 🐱

Perhaps you needed to know me 30 years ago as I don't look much like this now!!

It's a Sin – It's a S in (a pub)!!!!
Steve Colin

♫ Stevie's Puuuuuzzles
(and last Week's Answers)
of the Week ♫ ♟

This Edition's Quiz (only a few linked to elsewhere) –

▶ Cricket - A fitting tribute to Sir Tom, who was a big cricket fan, is the recent form of another Captain. Joe Root scored over 600 runs in 3 innings recently. Why does Joe Root use the number 66? A clue is not linked to above in the Texas story.

▶ What is special about last week's date 12 Feb 21, but not today's 21 Feb 21?

▶ What is the lowest composite number? See also 'Under the RADAR' below.

And some riddles too:

▶ I am a word that begins with the letter I. If you add the letter A to me, I become a new word with a different meaning, but that sounds exactly the same. What word am I?

▶ A man is washing windows on the 25th floor of an apartment building. Suddenly, he slips and falls. He has nothing to cushion his fall and no safety equipment—but he doesn't get hurt. How is this possible?

▶ What rock group consists of four famous men, but none of them sing? There is a clue elsewhere in this edition (sort of).

► A big black dog is standing in the middle of a big black road. There are no street lights above the road. An old black car with broken headlights is travelling towards the dog at 80mph but turns just in time before he hits the dog. How did the driver avoid the dog in time?

Last Edition's Answers -

► What can you never answer yes to? **Are you asleep!!**

► What gets bigger the more you take away. A hole.

► What always ends everything? 'G'. Not marriage, as DG said!! Funny, I got the same response from his wife. It's the only 'thing' they have ever agreed on!!

► I shave every day (obviously, not me!!!). Who am I? A barber.

Under the RADAR
(Random Alert Detailing Alternative Reports).

Stories you may have missed ...

Composite Number (see above) from a question on the chase - https://www.thesun.co.uk/tv/14063286/the-chase-mark-labbett-maths-composite-number-bradley-walsh/

Tom Thumb has a 28000 BMI. https://www.

theguardian.com/uk-news/2021/feb/18/6cm-tall-man-offered-covid-vaccine-after-nhs-blunder-liam-thorp

Next Week –

- ► TV – It's worth mentioning a few things that, if missed, you can catch up on 'catch up' –

As well as Trump vehicles mentioned above, others worth watching are:

- » Stan And Ollie – iPlayer
- » Trump Show – see above – iPlayer
- » In the Line of Duty (on Saturdays and iPlayer … all series available before new series due to start)
- » It's A Sin (as above) – All 4

Next Week's TV

- » Bringing up Baby. Monday 22nd Feb. BBC2 1 pm
- » Shallow Grave – Film 4 Tuesday 9 pm
- » The African Queen – Fri 26th Feb 6.50 pm Sony Movies

Next Edition – Kim and Kanya split up, I believe!!!! What a Travesty!!!!!! Focus next time, perhaps!!!!!! NOT!!!!

'See ya' soon. Stay safe and take care.

Steve

(‿|‿) **X1** Arnie's favourite Christian festival – he said to me, 'You have to love Easter, baby.' 😄

(‿|‿) **X2** A variation of why I stopped my chicken dating business – I couldn't make hens meet. 😄

(‿|‿) **X3** I often like to impress people by putting the pedal down all the way, but apparently, many people have seen me open a kitchen bin like that before. 😄

(‿|‿) **X4** Taxi for...??? I'm not sure if everyone is familiar with this phrase. When someone makes a fool of themself, shout taxi for (then surname). *A man called Mr Parker falls over a root of a tree ... His friend says, "Taxi for Parker!"*

(‿|‿) **X5** My grandad was also a Texan and used to own a kebab shop. When he passed away, we buried all the equipment with him. I bet he's still turning in his grave over this. 😄

(‿|‿) **X6** The "lone star" symbolises the solidarity of Texans in their declaration of independence from Mexico, and actually pre-dates the state flag (the details behind which can be found here.) Hence the state's official nickname became "The **Lone Star** State."

Issue No 31
Tuesday 23rd March 2021

MY BIRTHDAY – A YEAR ON!!!!!!
Happy Annivirusey!!!

Headlines:
- ► 'I've lost who I was': UK pauses to reflect on year of Covid
- ► Nicola Sturgeon vows to focus on elections after being cleared by inquiry

Leeds Utd Update - Fulham 1-2 Leeds, Fri 19th Mar
(Leeds are safe!!!)

The next issue is out soon. 'Coming out of Lockdown,' perhaps??!!

Hi all ... CCC is attached for your pleasure when you see this sign. 😊

In this Issue –
- ► Happy Birthday/Annivirusey to Me/Thee!!
- ► Birthday Cards (x3) from Mam!!
- ► Who's Who?? New Feature. Can You Name the Person????
- ► Stevie's Quiz - ONLY Last Edition's Answers
- ► A Year On - 'When Will We Be Safe?!'
- ► (Nothing) Under the RADAR (Random Alert Detailing Alternative Reports)

- Next Week's TV
- (‿|‿)(‿|‿)(‿|‿)

Happy Birthday/Annivirusey to Me/Thee!!

Further good news. A 'quick' one this edition to mark a very special day (i.e. my actual/official Birthday) and a year on from the start of the virus.

I hope you all 'observed' (‿|‿) **X1** a minute's silence to reflect my birthday. 😄

All together now … 👬

🎵 Happy Birthday/Annivirusey to me/thee

Happy Birthday/Annivirusey to me/thee

Happy Birthday/Annivirusey dear Stevie/Covid Vee

Happy Birthday to me/thee 🎵 😄

Apologies, but don't forget; I AM in court next week for being egotistical … but, I am appealing. 😄

Birthday Card(s) x3 from Mam/Mum

I got my birthday card off my 'mummy' today (sic). She is a very special person but is also quite old school and weird in the nicest possible way. Especially when it comes to birthdays and cards!!!

She started the conversation off by saying, 'I'm not sending any more birthday cards as they're too much hassle.' She insists on sending cards (not texts, WhatsApps, etc.) but spends an enormous amount of time deciding on the 'message/sentiment' and the look of the card, etc.

On this occasion, she then carried on to say, 'Having said that, I bought you two cards this year but decided to give you this one. So, that means you will have to have the other one next year as both, of course, say 'Son'.'

She continued, 'I also bought Michael (my brother) one for earlier in the month but decided it wasn't appropriate. So, you'll have to have that one the year after!!!'

Only Mam could start with 'not sending any more cards for birthdays' ... and finish with, 'I've got your next 3.' 😄

Who's Who?? Name the Person (New Feature!!!!!!!)

In a brand-new feature, I'll give you a few clues to a person's identity and see if you can name him or her. 🐱

Clue No 1 –

▶ Driving down York Road (in Leeds) one day, the car up behind was 'tailgating' and this person said ... 'He was right up my a**e and, do you know, I would have slammed on my brakes and let him crash into the back of me, BUT I wasn't insured, and my car wasn't MOT'd' at the time.'

😄

Clue No 2 –

► At another time, when their car was not insured and MOT'd, this person was stopped by the police and asked to take relevant documents into the station asap. They decided to go at the time of the Leeds Music Festival as they thought that most of the main staff would be there and not at the station checking documents (or the ones who were, would not be very 'alert'). The individual left the station disappointed that 'the Bright B**ch' behind the counter noticed the out-of-date documents. 😅

Clue No 3 –

► During the mega-search into finding the 'missing' child Shannon Mathews, this person was stopped for using a mobile phone whilst driving and given an on-the-spot fine and three points. Their response to the police was … 'Shouldn't you be out doing some real policing and finding Shannon Matthews?' 😂

Clue No 4 –

► Speeding down the motorway with six-month-old daughter in the back seat of the car. This person was stopped by the police after a police car appeared from behind a 'grassy knoll' (probably my embellishment, but I'm not sure after so many years). Police asked said person to sit in the police car and was shared earlier footage of the car speeding past and was asked, 'What was that? Can you identify that car?' Their genuine (and I believe without sarcasm) response was … 'Sorry, how can you expect me to do that at the speed that car was travelling?' 😂

Clue No 5 (That's enough clues, Steve) …

… 'Answers on a postcode'/by email, please. 🙈🙈

Next Week – a new Who's Who (and, perhaps, I need a new title for the section) … or maybe just do more of the same as there's plenty to go at with this person. 😂

🎵 Stevie's Puuuuuzzles
(and Last Week's Answers)
of the Week 🎵 🙈

This Edition's Quiz (Given the Who's Who (above), only answers from last time in this slot) –

▶ Cricket – A fitting tribute to Sir Tom was a big cricket fan is the recent form of another Captain. Joe Root scored over 600 runs in 3 innings recently. Why Does Joe Root use the number 66?
  It's nothing to do with Route 66, apparently, but (coincidentally) his first major innings

score!!!

▶ What is special about last week's date 12 Feb 21, but not today's 21 Feb 21?
It is palindromic (as many got) BUT also an ambigram. Back to front and upside down - just like we all feel like atm!! See below.

▶ What is the lowest Composite Number?
4. See also 'Under the RADAR' below.

And some riddles too:

▶ I am a word that begins with the letter I. If you add the letter A to me, I become a new word with a different meaning, but that sounds exactly the same. What word am I?
Isle/Aisle

▶ A man is washing windows on the 25th floor of an apartment building. Suddenly, he slips and falls. He has nothing to cushion his fall and no safety equipment, but he doesn't get hurt. How is this possible?
He is inside!!

▶ What rock group consists of four famous men, but none of them sing? Mount Rushmore. A link with Route 66 this time!!!

▶ A big black dog is standing in the middle of a big black road. There are no street lights above the road. An old black car with broken headlights is travelling towards the dog at 80mph but turns just in time before he hits the dog. How did the driver avoid the dog in time?

It was daylight!!!!

A Year On - 'When Will We Be Safe?!'

Finally, I was out for a walk today when I bumped into a mate and his missus. Apparently, they'd been having a chat whilst out walking, and he said, 'When do you think we'll be safe?' His wife replied, 'Yes, I know what you mean, being able to see everyone, not having to wear masks, going out with mates and not having to think about CV constantly, etc.'

'No,' my mate said. 'When will Leeds Utd be safe of relegation and certain of staying up in the Prem League?' A Classic. 😄

Final (unrelated) thought. **Was it a coincidence that the Masked Singer (ITV show) came to our screens as I assume it was commissioned before CV-19?** 🎭

Under the RADAR (Random Alert Detailing Alternative Reports)

Stories you may have missed …

▶ Surely there's already enough for you this week? Back next edition!!

Next Week's TV

▶ Creed. Paramount – 9-11.45 pm, Wed 24th March
▶ La La Land. BBC1 – 11.35 pm-1.35 am, Friday 26th March

'See ya' soon. Stay safe and take care.... .

Steve

(⌣|⌣) **X1** A minute's silence. Why do we say this? Does it just mean just to do something without speaking and show respect? To **observe** something in this context has the sense given in this entry: "To celebrate duly, to solemnise in the prescribed way (a religious rite, ceremony, fast, festival, etc.)." The concept of obedience is related -- you are obeying the protocol that calls for silence -- but we cannot say that you are obeying the time itself.

Answers

► If there is a conflict in Ukraine and a plane crashes on the border of Ukraine and Russia. In which country will they bury the survivors?

Answer: You don't bury survivors.

Issue No. 36

Star Trek Joke Answers (I'm sure you got most of them)
► How does a Romulan frog stay camouflaged? **He uses a croaking device!**
► What did Mr Spock find in Captain Kirk's toilet? **The Captain's Log!**
► How many ears does Captain Kirk have? **Three. A right ear, a left ear and a final front ear!**
► What is Commander Riker's favourite hobby? **Sewing, because Captain Picard is always saying, "Make it so!"**
► Where do the Borg go to eat fast food? **Borger King!**
► What's it called when a crew member on Deep Space 9 runs as fast as he can? **Worf Speed!**
► What are glasses called on planet Vulcan? **Spocktacles!**
► How do you stop yourself from falling out of a

Bird of Prey? **You have to Klingon!**

▶ What do you call two science officers having an argument? **Science Friction!**

▶ If Spock has pointy ears, then what does Scotty have? **Engineers!**

▶ Why is Star Trek so successful? **Because it has good Genes!**

▶ What illness did everyone on the Enterprise catch that made them red and itchy? **Chicken Spocks!**

▶ Why did Riker die from friendly fire? **Because Picard ordered "Fire at Will!"**

▶ What did Scotty say when little shards of ice began hitting the Enterprise? **"Captain, we are being hailed!"**

▶ Why was Captain Picard so confused when the android disappeared? **Because they'd lost their Data!**

Issue No. 35

No 1 – Sporting Theme Tunes 👥

▶ Sporting Themes. Let me know your Top 3 Favourite Sporting TV Theme Tunes. Will your pick agree with our 'Esteemed' Panel? } **Grandstand, Pot Black and Test Match Special**

No 2 – 10 Reasons Beer Piles on the Pounds 👥

▶ An Easy One – Why do we put weight on when

we drink beer/alcohol? **Can we get to a list of 10?** I have 6. I'll start with an easy one. Beer itself is calorific.

Eat more before (to line stomach), during (snacks) and after (when get in and next morning as inhibitions are low). What's the point of trying to diet if drinking all this!!!

Issue No. 34

Chickens or Dickens Quiz Answers

1.   **Brownlow – Dickens.** Mr Brownlow befriends Oliver after he is charged with pickpocketing. He later establishes Oliver's true identity and adopts him in **Oliver Twist.**

2.   **Australorp – Chickens.** The Australorps are a favourite in many Australian backyards due to their brilliant black, white or blue plumage, eggceptional egg laying talents and their characteristic happy-go-clucky Aussie attitude.

3. Pecksniff – Dickens. Seth is a sanctimonious surveyor and architect in **Martin Chuzzlewit**. He "has never designed or built anything," and is one of the biggest hypocrites in fiction. Father of daughters Mercy and Charity. In an effort to gain old Martin's money, he embraces then throws out young Martin at old Martin's wish. When long-time servant Tom Pinch learns of Pecksniff's treachery, he is also thrown out. Pecksniff's self-serving designs are eventually exposed by old Martin, who reconciles with his grandson, young Martin. Dickens' description of Pecksniff's hypocrisy is telling. "Some people likened him to a direction-post, which is always telling the way to a place, and never goes there."

4. Bagnet – Dickens. A musical and military family headed by Matthew, an old army friend of George Rouncewell. Bagnet's wife, the old girl, knows Matthew so well that he always calls upon her to supply his opinion. The Bagnet children Quebec, Malta, and Woolwich, are named after the military bases where the family has been stationed. Matthew is the guarantor of George's loan from Smallweed. When Smallweed calls in the debt, George is forced to deliver a document Smallweed needs to help lawyer Tulkinghorn learn Lady Dedlock's secret in **Bleak House.**

5. Barnevelder – Chickens. The Dutch-bred Barnevelder breed has to be one of the most popular, distinctive and attractive types of backyard chickens in Australia.

6. Isa Brown – Chickens. The ISA Brown is a humble chook. The name ISA Brown is not actually a breed name but a copyrighted brand name. The breed was developed and patented by a French company in 1978 for optimum egg production, and since then, its popularity has grown to great heights.

7. Swiveller – Dickens. Dick Friend of Fred Trent, Swiveller has designs to marry Fred's sister, Nell Trent, but is encouraged to wait until Nell has inherited her grandfather's money. When Nell and her grandfather leave London, Swiveller is befriended by Quilp, who helps him gain employment with the Brasses. While at the Brasses, he meets their little half-starved servant, whom he nicknames "the Marchioness." He becomes aware of the Brasses' villainy and, with the Marchioness' help, exposes a plot to frame Kit Nubbles. Swiveller later inherits money from his aunt, puts the Marchioness through school, and ultimately marries her in **The Old Curiosity Shop**.

8. Orpington – Chickens. Created by British poultry breeders at the turn of the 20th century, the Orpington chicken was designed to be a hardy breed that can endure England's most bitter winters, whilst still laying at an unstoppable rate.

9. Frazzle – Chicken. Frizzle chicken is a curious-looking chook with a warm temperament and a surprising amount of grit for someone so glamorous. To the untrained eye, the Frazzles look like they've been blown dried!

10. Chuzzlewit – Dickens. Martin, grandson of Martin Sr., has a falling out with his grandfather over his love for Mary Graham. He becomes a pupil of Pecksniff, who, because of pressure from the grandfather, throws young Martin out. After a trip to America with Mark Tapley, he comes back to England. After the undoing of Pecksniff, he reconciles with his grandfather and marries Mary Graham in **Martin Chuzzlewit**.

11. Leghorn – Chickens. Leghorn chickens are adventurous, spirited and excellent egg-layers. Developed in Tuscany, they came to the UK in the late 1800s.

12. Pumblechook – Dickens. Mr is Joe Gargery's uncle ("but Mrs Joe appropriated him") in **Great Expectations**. Conceited and utterly materialistic, he is a "well-to-do corn-chandler in the nearest town, [with] his own chaise-cart." He takes Pip on his first meeting with Miss Havisham and gives himself all the credit for arranging Pip's change in fortune.

13. Sebright – Chicken. Unique and exotic-looking ladies with sweet temperaments and a penchant for curiosity. In the early 1800s, Sir John Sebright – a member of the British Parliament and avid animal keeper – set out to create his vision of a perfect chicken.

14. Buckeye – Chicken. A dual purpose hen that thrives in the cold! The Buckeye chicken has the distinction of being the only breed to have been created by a woman.

15. Bantam – BOTH Chickens and Dickens! Bantam, Angelo Cyrus is the Master of Ceremonies at a ball in **The Pickwick Papers**.

Issue No. 33

1. You have to take a tablet every ½ hour … How long does it take to take three tablets?

1 hour only

2. How many animals of each species did Moses take aboard the Ark?

Zero, it was Noah

3. How many months of the year have 28 days?

All of them

4. You are in a square house, and every wall faces south … you come out of the door and see a bear … what colour is it?

White. It is at the North Pole

5. A farmer has 17 sheep, and all but nine die … how many are left?

Nine

6. You are driving a bus from Inverness to Newquay. The first stop is Newcastle and picks

up 2 customers, then stop at Leeds and pick up a mother with her two sons. Then final stop at Birmingham and pick up two adults. What is the name of the bus driver?

Whatever your name is ... 'You' are the driver.

7.   You are taking part in a race. You overtake the second person. What position are you in?

Second

8.   If you overtake the last person, then you are …?

How can you?

9.   Take 1000 and add 40 to it. Now add another 1000. Now add 30. Add another 1000. Now add 20. Now, add another 1000. Now add 10. What is the total?

4100

10. Mary's father has five daughters: 1. Nana, 2. Nene, 3. Nini and 4. Nono. What is the name of the 5th daughter?

Mary

Issue No. 33

Who's Who Answer ... Uncle John

Issue No. 32

▶   What goes around the world but stays in one corner?

   A stamp

▶   What two words have the most letters?

Post office

► What word begins with and ends in 'n' and means constipation?

Nnnnnnnnnnnnnnnnnn

Issue No. 31

Who's Who Answer ...

If you know him, you'll have guessed it, and there was plenty more to go at!!!

It would be indiscreet to name him here but what I will say is that his name begins with R ... and ends in ... oss Higham. 😁

St. Gemma's Hospice

As mentioned previously, all proceeds from the release of this book will go to St. Gemma's Hospice. As you read in Issue No. 40, St Gemma's Hospice was the charity we raised funds for by doing the Three Peaks Challenge in memory of my brother.

Based in Moortown, Leeds, St. Gemma's Hospice has been providing expert care to the people of Leeds for over 40 years. For more information, including how to make a donation, visit their website or give them a call.

https://www.st-gemma.co.uk/
0113 218 5500